THE SPACE WITHIN
Interior Experience as the Origin of Architecture

Robert McCarter

REAKTION BOOKS

Published by Reaktion Books Ltd
Unit 32, Waterside
44–48 Wharf Road
London N1 7UX, UK
www.reaktionbooks.co.uk

First published 2016
Transferred to digital printing 2020
Copyright © Robert McCarter 2016
All images by and © the Author

Printed and bound in Great Britain
by CPI Group (UK) Ltd, Croydon CR0 4YY

A catalogue record for this book is available from the British Library

ISBN 978 1 78023 660 5

Contents

The interior experience of the worshippers shapes the space, structure, natural light, acoustics and orientation of the sanctuary. Alvar Aalto, Wolfsburg Church, Germany, interior of sanctuary; sketch made on 29 September 1983.

Introduction
The Primacy of Interior Experience in Architecture

Throughout human history interior space and its experience has served as both the beginning, the initial inspiration, for the design of architecture, and the end, the final purpose of architecture as it is engaged in inhabitation. Since the beginning of the Modern period, and continuing today, pivotal discoveries in architectural design may be traced back to a generative ideal of intimate interior experience, and the quality of the interior spatial experience of the inhabitants may be shown to be both the primary determinant of the architectural design process and the means of appropriately evaluating a work of architecture after it is built. This book explores how interior space has been integral to the development of Modern architecture from the late 1800s to today, and how generations of architects have engaged with interior space and its experience in their design processes, enabling them to fundamentally transform the traditional methods and goals of architectural composition. For many of the most recognized and respected architects practising today, the conception of the interior spatial experience continues to be the necessary starting point for design. Making rooms for inhabitation remains the primary reason to construct works of architecture.

Let's begin at the beginning of the process of conceiving and constructing architecture. The initial conception of an architectural work has most often originated with what Frank Lloyd Wright called 'the space within'. Spatially innovative rooms have emerged earlier in the design process, and are more powerful in their experiential impact, than the exterior forms that are eventually deemed appropriate to wrap or clad them. Yet in order to make the case for the primacy of the interior experience today, we need to counter our contemporary cultural and social obsession with exterior views and forms in the representation of architecture, and to highlight our obsessive focus on the exterior form, and our concomitant blindness to interior experience. As opposed to the distancing effect of the purely visual experience of looking at the exterior form of a building, placing it in front of us as an object for aesthetic speculation, in our embodied experience of an interior space, the room literally surrounds us, engaging all our senses – touch, hearing, smell, taste and vision – creating the feeling of embodied, haptic intimacy and bringing things near to us.

What have been recognized as the three most influential spatial 'discoveries' of early Modern architecture – still in use today and ordering contemporary works – all began with an inspiration about interior spatial experience. Frank Lloyd Wright's 'woven plan', a layering of the floor and ceiling that related directly to the East Asian concepts of the ground platform and the roof canopy, was first articulated in designs whose exterior appearance gives no indication whatsoever of the dynamic spatial structure existing within. In Adolf Loos's *Raumplan* (room plan), each room had its own proportions and position in section and was closely interrelated to the other rooms of the house, resulting in plans that were fractured into multiple levels, a kind of interior terrain or topography. In Le Corbusier's *plan libre* (free plan), the floor plane was occupied by freely curving walls, which formed interior spaces that fluctuated in their relationship to each other as the inhabitant moved through them on the *promenade architecturale* – an interior conception par excellence.

A shared characteristic of the majority of spatial concepts emerging in the early Modern movement is that they were all developed in opposition to the then-dominant manner of designing buildings of the École des Beaux-Arts, wherein the paths of the eye and the body, in following the movement route to the destination, are exactly the same. Yet when the eye and the body are equally engaged, the eye and the visual sense invariably dominate the experience, overpowering the other, subtler senses, including the synthetic, haptic sense of bodily position in space. In counterpoint to this visual-centric approach, in early Modern buildings the path of the eye and the path of the body are different. Rather than seeing and moving along the same central axis through the same sequence of spaces, the inhabitant meanders in plan and section through the interior spaces of the building; the resulting simultaneous perception of the spaces from varied viewpoints was shared with contemporary Cubist painting.

The tradition of architecture defined as interior space is one where the building may be said to be conceived not as an exterior form, but as an outer surface of interior space – the interior 'skin' of the inhabited room – in which the building allows the interior place of experience and inhabitation to unfold within the limits and boundaries set by the outer forms. The rooms within these boundaries were reconceived and redefined by Louis Kahn as 'a society of spaces', alluding to the way in which the rooms not only accommodate specific uses and functions but make places for unplanned meetings and chance encounters, the generators of social and cultural relations. This conception recognizes that in the end the most important 'function' of any building is to enrich experience and enhance the life that takes place within it.

The interior experience of rooms that are composed of a nesting of spaces is at once intimate and immense, connecting us to the cosmos at the same moment as it grounds us in the tactile touch. Attentiveness to both intimacy and immensity may be said to characterize the modern architects whose works remain in our memory due to their acute sensitivity to the subtleties of experience. This results from architects being deeply involved in the design of interior spaces that possess the quality of both immensity, connecting us to earth and sky and distant horizon, and intimacy, surrounding us with appropriately scaled surfaces and details that we engage at first hand, and which impart to immense spaces an intimate, embodied scale.

The way architecture makes room for experience and memory is exemplified in rooms that provide their inhabitants with a simultaneous sense of extending to the distant horizon and withdrawing into close places of repose; in rooms anchored to their sites and thereby integrated into the history and nature of their place; in rooms resonant with the memory of their making, legible in their structure, materials and joinery; in rooms brought to life by the play of light throughout the day, the season and the year; and in rooms tailored precisely to the rituals of daily life that take place within them. In their recognition of the primacy of the experience of the interior room, and its importance as the setting for the daily rituals and events of life, architects are paralleled by Modern writers, as indicated by the way rooms shape the lives and memories of authors, and the characters portrayed in literature.

It may seem paradoxical at first mention, but the interior experience of the exterior environment is a critical aspect of this conception of interior primacy in architecture. Architects whose interior spaces remain in our memory have invariably been acutely sensitive to the local climate, the constant change of the seasons and natural light, and the larger environment in which the building is placed, and how these may be engaged to enrich the experience of the inhabitants in the space within. Aldo van Eyck believed that all inhabited rooms – even exterior rooms – are fundamentally interiors, and held that all spaces designed by mankind, inside or outside, rooms or streets, are fundamentally conceived and experienced as interior spaces. Architecture that lasts is an interior that is grounded in its place, that uses minimal resources and has minimal impact on the environment, and that provides maximal engagement with its environment and maximal enrichment of experience for its inhabitants.

The only appropriate way to evaluate architecture is through our experience of it, with particular emphasis on the occupation of interior space, the methods and materials of its construction, and their interrelationship. Yet while the interior experience of buildings is all that matters to those who inhabit buildings, today it is seemingly of less and less interest to many of those who design those same buildings. It is the contention of this book that architectural design must be re-grounded and redefined as primarily about the interior space and its experience, what it is like to live inside a building, and not about what the exterior form looks like from the outside. In this understanding, architecture is primarily concerned not with what a building looks like, but with how a building's spaces are ordered to house the activities that take place within it; how a building engages its place and the history of human occupation that has taken place there; how a building is built, how it is structured and of what materials it is made; and how all these affect what is experienced by those who inhabit it. Today we need to rediscover the ancient insight that the interior experience of inhabitation is both the beginning and initiation of architectural design, as well as the end and evaluation of every work of architecture.

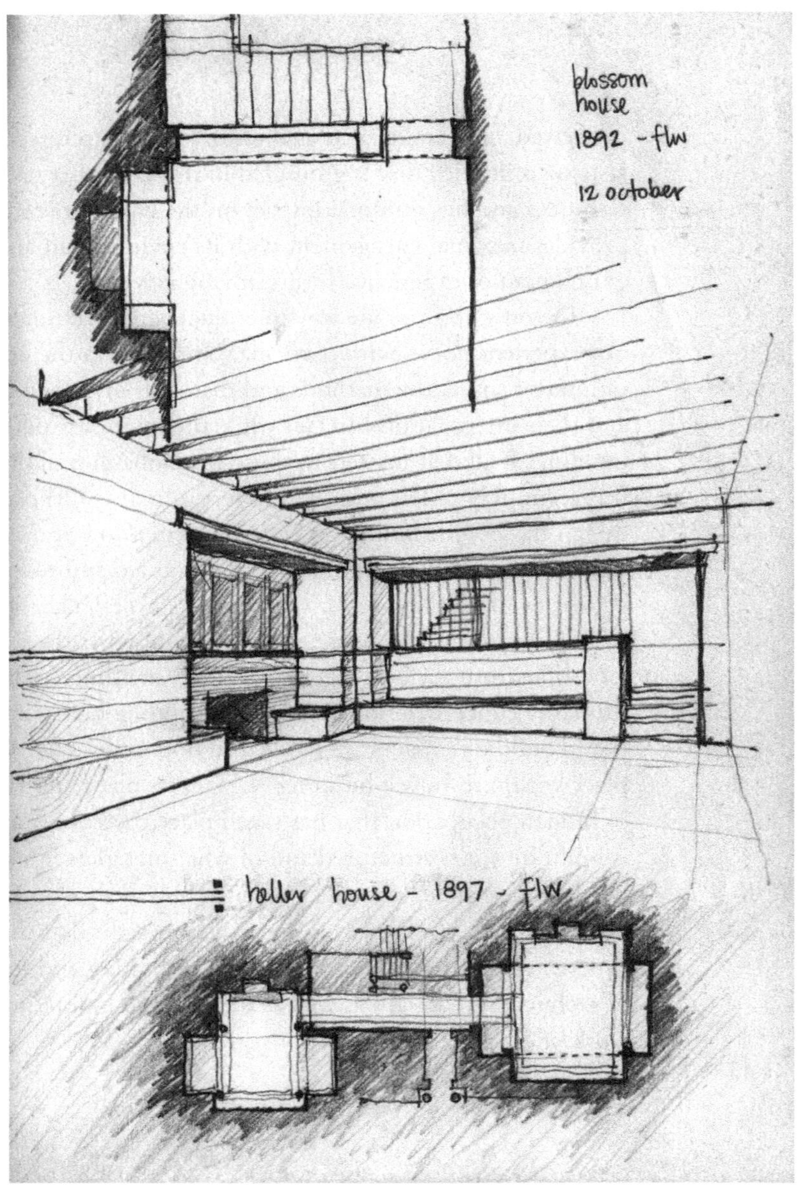

The development of early Modern spatial volumes and experiential qualities, including re-entrant corners and cruciform floor plans, within buildings characterized by traditional exterior forms. Frank Lloyd Wright, Blossom House, Chicago, Illinois, analysis of central stair hall and floor plan (top and centre), and Frank Lloyd Wright, Heller House, Chicago, Illinois, analysis of floor plan (bottom); sketch made on 12 October 1985.

One

The Space Within as the Origin of Architecture

Since the beginning of architecture, spatially innovative rooms have emerged earlier in the design process, and have been more powerful in their experiential impact, than the exteriors that are eventually deemed appropriate to clothe them. Prime early historical examples of spaces defined almost entirely as interior rooms would include the carved, cave-like temple spaces on the island of Malta, in Etruscan tombs in Italy and in rock-cut temples at Ajanta, India, and Abu Simbel in Egypt, all of which are composed of interior spaces with no exterior form other than the entry facade in the hillside. These ancient carved spaces are paralleled by constructed spaces that, while built and not excavated, are nevertheless also experienced as being carved interior spaces, including the almost entirely interior labyrinths of the Palace of Knossos at Crete and the city of Mycenae in ancient Greece. A number of these examples were created by cultures with matriarchal leadership structures, and the carved spaces on Malta have been described as 'womb-like' in experience, the enclosing and surrounding interior spaces best described by using female qualifiers.

Many other ancient buildings, while built on the ground and presenting exterior facades, reveal that actual embedment within the earth is not necessary for the construction of an all-encompassing interior experience. The nested spaces of almost complete darkness formed by the massive stonewalled buildings-within-buildings of the Temple of Horus at Edfu in Egypt were the most valued and sacred spaces of Egyptian society. Paradoxically complementing the Egyptian mass-shaped interiors are traditional Japanese buildings, lifted above the ground and constructed of lightweight wood frames and thin screens, which nevertheless form deep shadows and darkness in the domestic interior spaces within.[1] The greatest interior space-making culture remains the ancient Romans, as is epitomized by the Pantheon in Rome, where the massive, six-metre-thick wall, like a shell or mould, shapes the spherical volume of the interior space, which is anchored to the heavens by the central oculus marking the axis mundi, and to the earth by the convex floor forming the 'navel of the world'. This greatest of rooms makes present the ancient Romans' cosmological conception of the world as an interior space, and the life of mankind as taking place within it.

This emphasis on the primacy of interior space and its experience as the origin of architecture was also present at the very beginning of Modern architecture. Frank Lloyd Wright, whose work inspired and initiated what would later be called Modern architecture, believed that interior space – and not exterior form – was intractably bound up with direct experience and presence. Wright said that the architect's principal task was to build 'the room, the simple room', which he also called 'the space within', an insight he first articulated during the design of Unity Temple in 1906. In writing his *An Autobiography* in 1931–2, Wright noted:

> The interior space is the reality of the building. The room itself must come through or architecture has not arrived . . . Architecture not alone as form following function, but conceived as space enclosed. The enclosed space itself might now be seen as the reality of the building . . . The building now became a creation of interior space in light . . . This sense of the within, the room itself, I see as the great thing to be realized.[2]

In holding that the interior space 'must come through', that the exterior must be moulded to contain and present the interior space, Wright argued that the interior space must take shape prior to the exterior form – architecture must first be 'conceived as space enclosed'.

'The reality of the building does not consist in the four walls and the roof but in the space within to be lived in,'[3] Wright argued, paraphrasing a line from *The Book of Tea* by Okakura Kakuzō, which Wright first read while he lived in Japan in 1917–22. In furnishing his own homes in Wisconsin and Arizona, Wright often employed hollow vessels such as large pots and vases, with their useful enclosure of an interior volume, to complement the architecture around them. Wright's insights into the essence of both the room and the vessel are directly derived from Okakura's paraphrasing of the ancient Chinese poet and philosopher Lao Tzu (Laozi), who noted:

> Only in emptiness lay the truly essential. The reality of the room, for instance, was to be found in the vacant space enclosed by the roof and walls, not in the roof and walls themselves. The usefulness of a water pitcher dwelt in the emptiness where water might be put, not in the form of the pitcher or the material of which it is made. Emptiness is all potent because all containing. In emptiness alone motion becomes possible.[4]

The space within thus understood as enclosed room makes it possible for people to dwell, to live, to move and to enact the rituals of daily life. Wright's contemporary and fellow Chicagoan the American philosopher John Dewey defined architecture as the formation of interior space 'as opportunity for movement and action'.[5]

Wright's primary spatial concepts and principles of order, which are today recognized as important innovations in the emergence of Modern architecture, were first given built form through the definition and enclosure of inhabited interior spaces, and only much later given what Wright considered appropriate exterior form. While the exteriors of his early houses are typical for the era, the interiors are characterized by the open, interpenetrating spaces for which Wright's Prairie period architecture after 1902 would be praised, but in fact these qualities of 'the space within' were experienced by the inhabitants of these houses a full ten years earlier. The innovative spatial concepts to be found in the interiors of Wright's houses starting around 1890 may be experienced by anyone who visits the houses or studies their floor plans, yet the literature on Wright and his place in Modern architecture is almost entirely silent regarding the experiential qualities of the spaces within his early houses.

Wright's initial evolution of his spatial ideas on the interior is exemplified by a number of his early 'moonlight' houses – so-called because he designed them at home in the evenings after his day work in the office of Adler & Sullivan in Chicago – which dated from before Wright established his own practice in 1893. The exterior forms of the Emmond, Parker and Gale Houses, all of 1892, are typical of the Victorian domestic style, with gabled roofs, turreted towers and bay windows, and as a result they are only very rarely recognized as Wright designs. Yet the floor plans of all three houses are divided down their centres by a bearing wall, with kitchen and services on one side and three linked public rooms symmetrically disposed on the other. This is the 'tripartite' plan, already fully formed and built out in these three houses of 1892, which Wright would establish as one of the two primary plan types of the Prairie house, as first presented in the *Ladies' Home Journal* nine years later in 1901.

The McArthur house, built in 1892, has a traditional exterior form, with a massive barn-roof gable set above a bay-windowed entrance floor, and is quite similar to the other contemporary houses in various Victorian styles along the street. Yet the floor plan holds a surprise, for the freestanding fireplace stands between the entrance hall and dining room, with open passages on both sides connecting

the rooms into a single extended volume – exactly as would occur
sixteen years later in one of the most famous of Wright's Prairie
houses, the Robie House of 1908. Next door to the McArthur
House is the Blossom House, also built in 1892, and its pyramid-
roofed, square-massed volume appears from the exterior to be a
straightforward classical composition, with projecting corners and
recessed centre bays. The floor plan is a large square divided into
nine smaller squares, with the central bays of each side recessed to
form an inset cruciform. This cruciform-in-square would be one
of Wright's most important plan types of his Prairie period, and it
was employed fourteen years later in his design for Unity Temple
of 1906. Inside the Blossom House are early examples of several
spatial compositional concepts Wright would employ throughout
his career, including blocked central movement axes, overlapping
and interpenetrating rooms, freestanding screen walls that do not
reach the ceiling, and walls that fold inwards and then outwards to
form re-entrant corners. The folded wall allowed Wright to develop
spatial continuity within the interior volume, resulting in an open
plan that nevertheless is experienced as enclosing the inhabitants:
'I called it continuity. It is easy to see it in the folded plane.'[6]

The primacy of interior space and its experience is also
the foundation of the work of Le Corbusier, perhaps the most
influential architect of the Modern period. Le Corbusier shared
with Wright an admiration of the precision with which vessels
such as bottles and glasses served as an analogy for the space-
containing and experience-defining qualities of architecture.
Throughout his career, Le Corbusier divided his days between
painting in his studio and designing architecture in his office, and
many of the interior spatial concepts employed in his buildings
first emerged in his early Purist still-life paintings of bottles,
wine glasses, guitars and other hollow concave forms. From these
studies, Le Corbusier came to define architecture as a vessel of
space for inhabitation, and the house as a bottle-like volume to

contain the family. In his presentation of his Unité d'habitation apartment complex at Marseilles of 1946, Le Corbusier made a drawing of prototypical dwellings: 'The drawings show a few very simple objects a) the hut of a savage, b) the tent of a nomad, c) a bottle, and the other c) an apartment at Marseilles' – the apartment as the 'other bottle', equally defined by the space it contains. The apartments-as-bottles are independent of the skeletal structural frame of the building, and Le Corbusier calls the apartments 'bottles' and the building 'the bottle-rack', into which the apartment-bottles can be placed. Each apartment 'is a container, in this case an apartment which can be considered as a complete element: like a bottle'.[7]

In a statement remarkably similar to Wright's – and to Laozi's – Le Corbusier summarized his work on the Dominican monastery of La Tourette in 1959 with a definition of the space of inhabitation within architecture as being analogous to a hollow vessel: 'Architecture is a vase. My reward for eight years of labour [on La Tourette] is to have seen the highest things grow and develop within that vase . . . [The monastery] does not speak of itself. It lives on its interior. It is in the interior that the essential occurs.'[8] It was during this period that Le Corbusier's paintings ceased to engage the thin, transparent vessels depicted in the earlier still-lifes and began to engage more massive, organic, concave, hollow, space-enclosing volumes, such as seashells, bone sections and eroded stones, which he called objects 'à réaction poétique'. This was paralleled in his architecture by the increasing importance given to the emotional resonance of the interior space – what he called 'the ineffable space' – which was most often enclosed in thick walls and shaped as if having been carved or hollowed out.

In the initial conceptual designs for the chapel at Ronchamp of 1950, Le Corbusier described the building as a 'shell' enclosing the space of worship, and the study models of the design's curving walls and roof were made of paper on a wire frame, which glowed with inner light like a lantern. While the final building was made of massive rubble-filled walls and concrete roof, Le Corbusier felt the lantern-like models best presented the interior space. This mode of design was continued in the Philips Pavilion at the Brussels World's Fair of 1958, an interior space designed for experiencing the *poème électronique,* with music by Edgard Varèse and Iannis Xenakis (a composer-architect who worked in Le Corbusier's atelier). Le Corbusier generated the curved surfaces of the building in a process quite close to that of the sculptor Naum Gabo, as well as his own study models for Ronchamp, in which a frame is erected and closely spaced wires stretched to form the ruled surfaces that torque from vertical to horizontal and back again. Describing the pavilion as a 'bottle', Le Corbusier wrote: 'the exterior will be made only with scaffolding . . . the raison d'être is the interior.'[9]

The understanding that the conceptual origination of architectural design starts with the interior space, the room, also characterized the work of the second generation of Modern architects, most notably Louis I. Kahn. As had Wright, Kahn made the focus of his work the space within, and our inhabitation of it, stating: 'The room is the beginning of architecture.'[10] He believed that a room must reveal to those who inhabit it how it was built: 'But you want to see how [the room] is made, so therefore a space *does* show evidence of how it was made within the space itself – not just for enclosure alone, but for light that you want this space to have, the natural light.'[11] Kahn held that the architect should design spaces that were so appropriate to their intended occupation that inhabitants could intuit their use: 'Rooms must suggest their use without name.'[12] He also believed that the behaviour and experience of a room's inhabitants are profoundly affected by the character of the space: 'The room is so marvelous that its size, its dimension, its walls, its windows, its light – *its* light, not just light – have an effect on what you say and what you do.'[13] For Kahn, the construction of powerfully affecting rooms was the greatest achievement of architecture throughout history, and he often spoke of the Pantheon in Rome and the Baptistery in Florence, and how inhabiting them had changed him: 'So sensitive is a room.'[14] It was architecture's essence as interior experience of the room that convinced Kahn to change his university studies from art to architecture – the realization, as he said later, that architecture was 'an art you can . . . *be in*'.[15]

Many leading contemporary architects also emphasize the primacy of interior space in both design and experience. Steven Holl begins his designs with initiatory watercolour sketches, which most often present spaces seen from within, from the point of view of the inhabitant. In project after project, Holl conceives and documents the interior spaces before unfolding the plan, the overall building volume and, last of all, its exterior form. It was the watercolour sketches of the gallery interiors that convinced the jury for the Helsinki Contemporary Art Museum, Helsinki, that Holl had conceived them in their light, and the interior spaces of the completed building remain true to both the spirit and experiential qualities presented in his initial watercolours. In his initial design for the competition for the Nelson-Atkins Museum of Art in Kansas City, Holl made the watercolour view from the Isamu Noguchi sculpture room inside the museum out to the Dan Kiley-designed sculpture garden before making either the plan or section of the building; as Holl said, 'Once you've got a concept and a strategy, you work your way from the main interior spaces out to the building, because the inside is always more important than the outside.'[16]

The work of Tod Williams and Billie Tsien also exemplifies the primacy of interior space and its experience as the initial inspiration for conceiving the design, the determinant of the design development and its realization through construction, and the only valid means of evaluating the built work after its completion. They described what they value in a work of architecture, and what

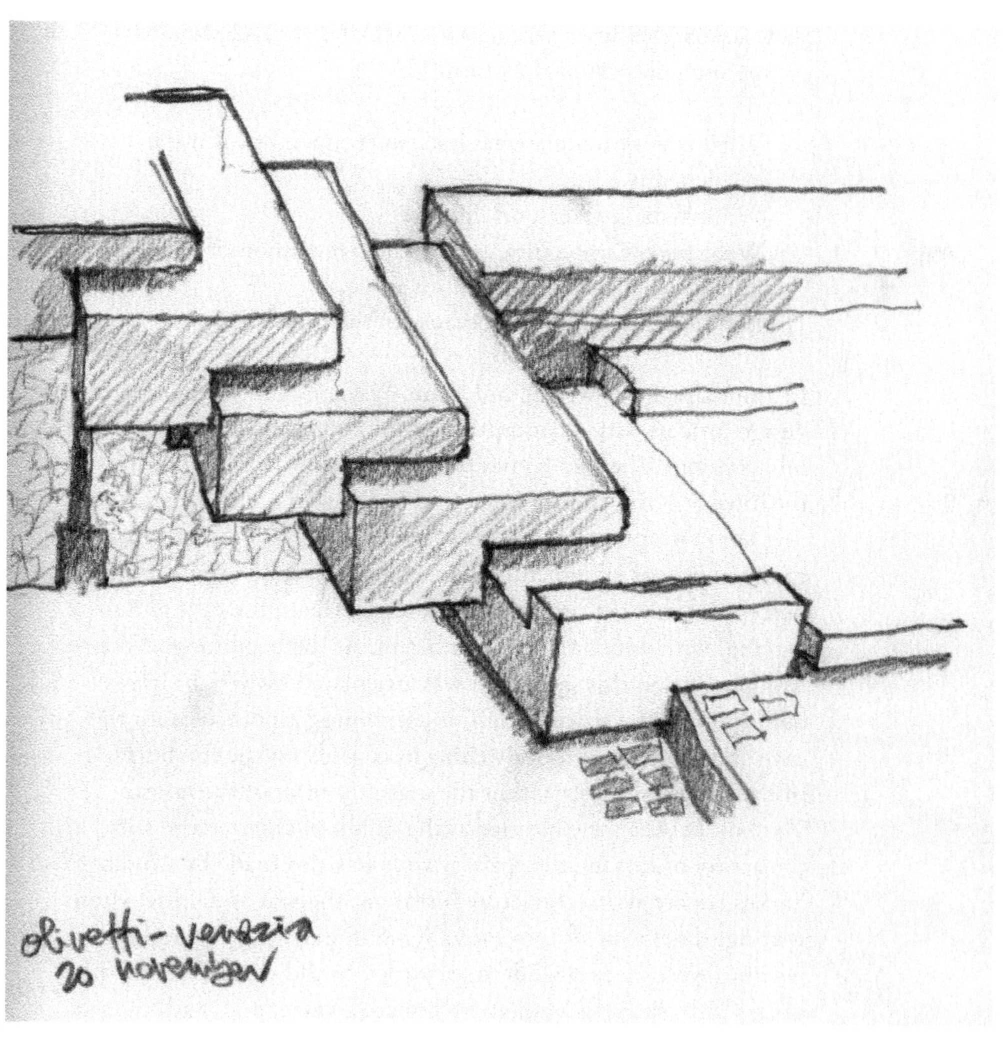

The celebration of the events of daily inhabitation, such as ascending a staircase from the ground to an upper level. Carlo Scarpa, Olivetti Showroom, Venice, Italy, interior detail of central staircase; sketch made on 20 November 2012.

they seek in their own work, as that which lasts and remains
as a permanent part of the lifeworld:

> What is important is what lasts, in the memory, if not in
>   actuality.
> What lasts is space and light.
> What lasts is ambiguity, and the slow revelation of materiality.
> Finally, what lasts is the interior space.
> Buildings are important because of the interior.[17]

In a similar way to Wright and Kahn, Williams and Tsien begin their
design process with a conception of the room, the interior space of
inhabitation: 'The idea comes from the interior. We live our lives in
the interior – the exterior is less and less important as we get older.'[18]

The conception of interior space as being far more essential
to the nature of architecture than exterior form has roots in the
perception that the origins of architecture lie in the cave and in
carving, with which the chapter began. At the beginning of the
Modern period this same idea was articulated by Wright in his
definition of 'the space within' as combining aspects of both the
cave and the tent, and of dwelling as centred on the fire burning
in the hearth set deep within the masonry mass of the house.
The link between the interior as the origin of architecture and
the action of carving the space within was also made by Adrian
Stokes, an art and architecture historian, theorist and critic whose
writings date from 1930 to 1967. While the majority of Stokes's
writings were on pre-Modern artworks, he did write on the works
of Le Corbusier and Modern architecture in general, and his critical writings were strongly influenced by his close friendships with
the painter Ben Nicholson and the sculptor Barbara Hepworth,
Modern artists who employed low relief carving in their works.

Stokes distinguished between modelling, the additive building
up of material to make a positive form, and carving, the subtractive

removal of material to make a negative space within the confines of the pre-existing solid form, and he asserted that the making of architecture is predominantly an action involving carving. 'Primitive dwellings are caves carved by the elements,'[19] Stokes noted, and he argued for the continued relevance of carving and its relation to space-making in architecture in the Modern period, stating that contemporary architecture and building are 'the source at which carving or spatial conception renews its strength'.[20] Stokes noted how the additive process of modelling was an act of creation through the projection and imposition of the designer's formal conceptions onto the material out of which it is made, or the place in which it is created, without any concern for their own inherent natures and characters. On the other hand, the subtractive process of carving was an act of construction, not creation, and in this way of evolving and unfolding the design, 'conception is all the time adjusted to the life' or nature of the material or place that the architect uncovers, resulting in a revelation of the space-shape latent in and inherent to the material or place.[21]

As Stokes defined it, modelling is focused on preconceived exterior form that is perceived almost exclusively through vision, and the materials preferred in modelling are plastic, have little character of their own and are capable of easily being formed into any shape desired. On the other hand, carving is focused on interior space discovered or disclosed in the process of making that is perceived by all the senses working in unison, and the solid and resistant nature of the carved materials is directly experienced in the largely tactile way 'we are compelled to feel our way into spaces'.[22] Referring to what he perceived to be the decline of the interior spatial values of carving, best experienced through embodied inhabitation, and the rise of the exterior plastic formal values of modelling, best experienced by sight alone, Stokes noted: 'Photographs transmit plastic values exceedingly well, carving values hardly at all.'[23]

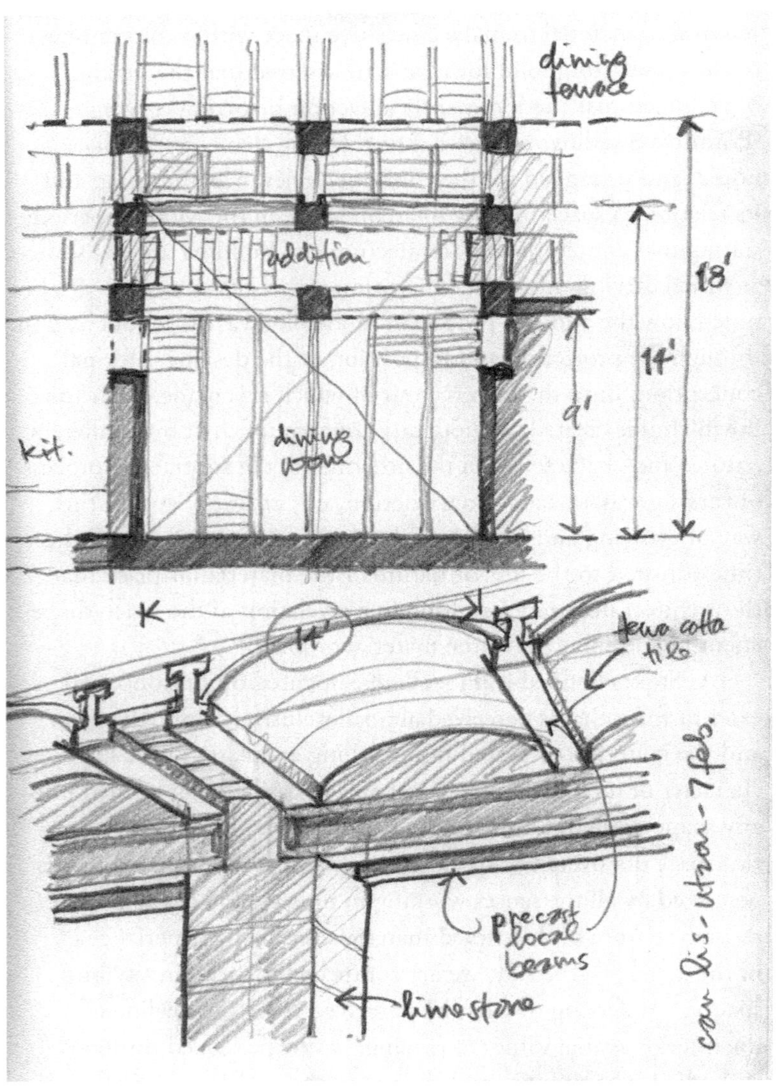

Interior intimacy of the dining room fixed into the fabric of the house by the exposure of construction and materials. Jørn Utzon, Can Lis, Mallorca, Spain, plan of dining room, with Utzon's later addition making the plan a square and providing doors to the terrace (top), and detail of ceiling and roof structure as seen from the dining room (bottom); sketch made on 7 February 2015.

Two

The Nearness of Interior Experience and the Distance of Exterior Form

In order to make evident the continued primacy of the interior experience in architecture today, it is necessary to counter our contemporary cultural and social obsession with exterior views and external forms in the representation of architecture. This has led to our experiencing a building solely as a freestanding object of aesthetic speculation, detached from its place in every way through its being disengaged from the particularities of the landform, the mood of the climate and the qualities of local cultural, social and building traditions. In parallel, it is also important to highlight the way that our focus on the exterior form invariably leads to our near total blindness to interior experience. In evaluating and knowing architecture, photographs of exterior forms are quite literally seen as the only 'reality', as reflected in the almost exclusive attention given to building exteriors by architectural historians, critics, educators and the profession itself. Of far greater importance is the way this obsession with the visual representation of the exterior forms of architecture dominates all types of media, from Internet postings to hard-copy publications, which shapes the general public's perception and understanding of architecture. We live in a time that seems to be dominated by images; a time when what a building looks like on the exterior is often all that matters in our evaluation of a work of architecture. We feel we 'know' architecture and the places it makes, both old and new, through

the photographs of buildings we see in magazines, books and
– ever more predominantly – online, without ever inhabiting
their spaces.[1]

On the other hand, Alvar Aalto, the Finnish architect, argued
that what mattered in architecture was not what a building 'looks
like' on the day it opens, but what it 'is like' to live in thirty years
later, and this valuation of what buildings were like to be in and
to experience over their exterior form is one of the founding
principles of Modern architecture.[2] Along with critics such as
Adrian Stokes, Frank Lloyd Wright argued that photographs
entirely failed to capture the true essence of architecture as it is
experienced, and that photographs were thus an inappropriate
way to represent architecture as seen from the exterior. When the
Larkin Building in Buffalo, New York, of 1904 was published in
an architectural journal in 1908 with a critique written by Russell
Sturgis, who never visited the building, and whose text was based
entirely on looking at photographs, Wright responded with a
sharply worded rebuttal. Wright's most scathing criticism was
directed at Sturgis's comments based on wide-angle photographs
of the exterior of the building taken from a third-storey window
of the factory across the street. Wright argued that a building must
be evaluated by its interior experience, and that the exterior, as
an expression of the interior, must be evaluated from the human
standing eye-level, stating that the qualities of a building can only
be known 'when you know the building *on the ground*.'[3]

Our increasing dependence on the photograph, rather than
our own memories, was highlighted by the artist and educator
Josef Albers shortly after leaving the Bauhaus in Dessau and
starting to teach at Black Mountain College in North Carolina
in 1933. Albers pointed out that the visual and spatial memory was
so poorly trained in general education, and thus in contemporary
society as a whole, that, while most people could easily recall a
tune they recently heard, very few could remember 'the extension

of space and volume' – the characteristics of the room they only recently occupied.[4] This general societal blindness to interior space, in both experience and memory, has certainly not improved in the years since Albers first noted it. Equally if not more troubling is the fact that, when one visits architecture schools today, it is rare indeed to find an architecture studio that is organized so as to have the students begin with the design of a room, and where the students' designs throughout the term are evaluated first as an interior experience, and only afterwards as an exterior form. In our exterior form-obsessed time, it has become a seemingly impossible task for architecture professors to keep the students' minds on the interior experience – even though in the end that is all that matters to the inhabitants of architecture.

Our societal obsession with the exterior form of buildings as the only attribute worthy of being recognized and attended to has led, as Albers suggested, to an attrition of our collective abilities to perceive the many characteristics and qualities of architectural experience that cannot be captured in a photographic image. Regarding this exterior focus of both the architectural profession and society at large, the educator and architect Wilfried Wang has noted:

> From education to professional practice, the majority of images of architecture that are received are determined by their degree of photogeneity; that is, the degree to which an image of a designed phenomenon can be reduced to a recognizable icon. Thanks to this 'cultivation' of the media . . . there are huge areas of the architectural design field that are completely neglected because the dominant discourse does not know how to address them. These areas of neglect are quotidian use; temporal changes that notably affect the quality of light and perceptions of landscapes; . . . and, at the other end of the scale, interiors and their interrelationships (because more than

the exterior of buildings, interiors are traversed, experienced through use and movement) as well as details.[5]

As a result of this tendency, when considering much contemporary architecture, one is often confronted by a seemingly irresolvable paradox, a dichotomous and ostensibly mutually exclusive pair of concepts between which one must choose: exterior form and interior place. While exterior form almost invariably devolves into the production of self-referential objects and surfaces, place-form may be said to emerge only from an engagement with the experiential lifeworld and recognition of the inherent interiority of inhabited space. That places are always fundamentally experienced as interiors, irrespective of whether they are outside or inside, was noted fifty years ago by the Dutch architect Aldo van Eyck: 'Architecture implies the creation of "interior" both outside and inside, for "exterior" is that which precedes man-made environment.'[6] It is clear that aestheticized object-forms are exclusively apprehended from what Van Eyck calls this 'exterior' point of view. The dichotomy of exterior form and interior place would appear to present a clear choice between opposite design determinants for contemporary architectural practitioners.

Yet Van Eyck's definition of all designed space, inside or outside, as being 'interior', as well as Wright's earlier principle that the exterior form is the result of 'the interior room coming through', suggest that such intractable dichotomies are not inherent in architectural design. The architectural historian David Van Zanten has argued that the nature of an architect's design process, by way of which an architectural design is realized, determines the characteristics of the resulting building. Van Zanten noted that the method of design taught at the École des Beaux-Arts during the time of Louis Sullivan and Wright, which is paralleled by the method of design employed by many International Style architects in Kahn's time, was in fact not a design process at all, but rather a predetermined compositional procedure, an 'art of command' in which the architect dictates the form of the building, based upon preconceived precedents, and in which the activities to be housed within the building, as well as the materials out of which it is made, have no effect on the design. On the other hand, Van Zanten held that Sullivan, Wright and Kahn practised the 'art of nurture', a process of design in which the architect seeks a fit between function and form, shaping the space to fit the human activity to take place within it, and in which the nature of the materials of which the design is made have significant effect on the design.[7] Van Zanten's 'art of nurture' closely parallels Stokes's definition of 'carving' as revealing the essence of what lies within, as opposed to 'modelling' as an imposition of predetermined form, and both may be characterized as doing what is appropriate: Kahn said, 'I teach appropriateness. I don't teach anything else.'[8]

As opposed to the distancing effect of the purely visual experience of looking at the exterior form of a building and placing it in front of us as an isolated sculptural object, in our experience of an interior space, the room literally surrounds us, engaging all our senses – touch, hearing, smell, taste and vision – creating a feeling of embodied, haptic intimacy. In 1894, well before the beginning of Modernism, Wright stated that architecture should fundamentally be defined as the making of 'a room to live in', and 35 years later he wrote that architecture was primarily involved with providing 'use and comfort' for its inhabitants: 'Human use and comfort should have intimate possession of every interior.'[9] Yet this seemingly straightforward and remarkably modest assertion has been ignored far more often than it has been honoured in modern times. If, as Wright argues, interiority is about the 'intimate possession' of the inhabited room, and the 'use and comfort' of the room's inhabitants, then it cannot also simultaneously be concerned primarily with the shape of the building's exterior.

Here it is important to recognize that a building is not the object of our focused attention, but rather, as Wright first noted in 1896, a work of architecture surrounds us and encloses us in the space within, thereby acting as the 'background or framework' in which the rituals of our daily lives take place.[10] Understood in this way, the interior space of architecture acts to shape and bring into presence our experience of inhabitation, allowing the human actions that take place to come forward, while the architecture recedes as the background or framework for our experience. This understanding was also shared by the cultural critic Walter Benjamin, who in 1936 argued that in everyday use architecture is typically experienced and perceived in 'a state of distraction', and is not the object of our focused optical attention, but rather is engaged through use, movement and touch – our haptic inhabitation of a familiar place:

> Buildings are appropriated in a twofold manner: by use and by perception – or rather, by touch (tactilely) and sight (optically). Such appropriation cannot be understood in terms of the attentive concentration of a tourist before a famous building. On the tactile side, there is no counterpoint to what contemplation is on the optical side. Tactile appropriation comes about not so much by way of attention as by way of habit. As regards architecture, habit determines to a large extent even optical reception of architecture, which . . . [takes its] cue from tactile appropriation – through habit.[11]

While the experience of the interior space of a room by definition engages all our senses as they are embodied in the haptic act of inhabitation, it is the sense of touch that creates tactile intimacy and, in doing so, brings things near to us. We refer to this as having things 'near at hand', within reach, and able to be easily touched, and the philosopher Martin Heidegger has written

The experience of the thermal bath takes place entirely within the thickness of the earth, in spaces carved out of the ground and covered over with grass. Peter Zumthor, Therme Vals, Switzerland, interior view and plan of central tepidarium pool; sketch made on 22 September 2004.

about the importance of this experience of nearness to our capacity
to dwell and be at home in the world. The sense of nearness has
to do with something being present, intimately occupying a space
with us, which Heidegger contrasts with the distance of the object
that 'stands before, over against, opposite us'. Paralleling Laozi,
Heidegger employs the hollow jug or vessel as the prime example
of a thing that is near to us because of 'the empty space' within it:
'The vessel's thingness does not lie at all in the material of which
it consists, but in the void that holds.'[12] Heidegger notes how the
space within the vessel, like the room in which it sits, brings
together the solid material of the earth and the open volume of
the sky. He suggests that we experience nearness most intensely
when we engage with all our senses, and gather together in
a place, a space bounded and enclosed.

The Finnish architect, educator and author Juhani Pallasmaa
has noted:

> The dominance of the eye and the suppression of the other
> senses tends to push us into isolation, detachment and
> exteriority . . . Modernist design has housed the intellect
> and the eye, but it has left the body and the other senses,
> as well as our memories and dreams, homeless.[13]

In Pallasmaa's succinct treatise on sensorial balance in architecture, *The Eyes of the Skin*, he points out: 'All the senses, including
vision, can be regarded as extensions of the sense of touch,' and
yet, when operating in isolation, 'the eye is the organ of separation
and distance, whereas touch is the sense of nearness, intimacy and
affection.'[14] Pallasmaa has noted that the visual experience of interior space tends to rely less on our focused vision and more on our
peripheral vision, giving us an intimate sense of our body being
enclosed and enfolded by the surrounding walls, floor and ceiling:

> The immediate judgment of the character of space calls
> for our entire embodied and existential sense, and that
> character is perceived in a diffuse and peripheral manner
> rather than through precise and conscious observation.[15]

Peripheral vision is most efficient in dim light, which is conducive to intimacy, while to see clearly with focused vision requires bright light, which tends to emphasize the distance between us and the objects and spaces at which we are looking. Pallasmaa noted the way 'Peripheral vision integrates us with space, while focused vision pushes us out of the space, making us mere spectators.'[16]

The primacy of interior space, and its relation to tactility, is directly related to the thinking and work of the Cubist painter Georges Braque. Braque showed a marked preference for that which is near to us, rather than that which is distant, and this led him to abandon the landscape for the still-life, the Cubist vehicle par excellence. Braque stated: 'Impelled by the desire to go further in the manifestation of space . . . I wanted to make touch a form of matter.'[17] This was motivated, as Braque said, by

> the desire that I have always had to touch things and not only
> see them . . . So I began to paint mainly still lifes, because in
> nature there is a tactile space, I'd say almost a manual space
> . . . If a still life isn't within reach of my hand, it seems to me
> that it ceases to be a still life, ceases to be affecting.[18]

Braque's choice of still-life objects followed directly: 'Musical instruments, considered as objects, were special in that a touch would bring them to life.'[19] Braque's painting is remarkably consistent in his pursuit of tactile reality, and he continually critiqued classical perspective because

> it ended up making tactile reality more distant, instead
> of rendering it more visible . . . We, following Cézanne, have
> implanted a perspective that brings objects within the reach
> of the hand . . . To bring things closer to the spectator's view,
> to encourage the communion of the tactile and the visible.[20]

Braque famously dismissed the notion of the importance of the particular object to be painted with the suggestive statement: 'I was unable to introduce the object until I had created the space for it.'[21] Braque emphasized the ground or space of the painting, rather than the figure or object, and he noted that this, too, was related to the idea of tactility: 'Visual space separates objects from each other. Tactile space separates us from objects.' Purely visual representation was not sufficient: 'It is not enough to make someone see what one has painted, one must also make him touch it.'[22] Thus the emphasis on touch, on the tactile, is complemented by the emphasis on space, the space where the painting takes place, which Braque called 'tactile space', and a tactile space that brings things near to us is an interior space where 'touch becomes a form of matter.'

In the section on space and architecture in his 1934 book *Art as Experience*, John Dewey drew the contrast between hearing as the sense that creates intimacy by bringing things near to us, and vision as the sense that distances us from the things we apprehend: 'The eye is the sense of distance . . . but sound itself is near, intimate [and] the ear is the emotional sense.'[23] On the other hand, the view of the exterior form of a building, best seen as an object illuminated by bright light, is dominated almost exclusively by our focused vision, placing the things we see at a distance. Dewey's thinking closely parallels that of his contemporary Wright, as is illustrated in the story of the siting of Wright's most famous house, Fallingwater, of 1938. The client, Edgar J. Kaufmann, was surprised to find that Wright had placed the house on the top of the waterfall, rather than across the stream.

While the location selected by Wright allowed the house a southern rather than a northern orientation – something that is critical for the comfort of the inhabitants in the mountain context – Wright also did not want the waterfall present merely as an image to be looked at from within the house. He told Kaufmann: 'I want you to live with the waterfall, not just look at it, but for it to become an integral part of your lives.'[24] Wright indicated the difference between hearing the waterfall – an intimate experience of being near – and simply looking at it – a formal, distant experience – in saying of Kaufmann: 'He loved the site where the house was built and liked to listen to the waterfall. So that was the prime motive of the design . . . and he lives intimately with the thing he loves.'[25]

In the context of the present study, it is intriguing to note that, according to its canonical histories, Modern architecture began with an almost exclusive focus on interior space, as is reflected in Sigfried Giedion's *Space, Time and Architecture* of 1941 and Bruno Zevi's *Architecture as Space* of 1948, both of which traced the history of architecture as the history of the evolution of the manipulation of interior space. Indeed, as the architectural historian and critic Kenneth Frampton has noted,

> Space has since [the 1890s] become such an integral part of our thinking about architecture that we are practically incapable of thinking about it at all without putting our main emphasis on the spatial displacement of the subject in time.[26]

Architecture is both constructed and inhabited, and yet it can be argued that the space obsession of the Modern polemic has acted to overshadow and obscure the embodied and enclosed experience of architecture, as well as the 'tectonic culture', as Frampton named it, required to construct spatial enclosure.

In 1894 the architectural theorist August Schmarsow published *The Essence of Architectural Creation*, which presented the history of architecture as entirely determined by the evolution of man's ability to perceive space. That same year the poet Paul Valéry wrote: 'What we call space is relative to the existence of whatever structures we may choose to conceive. The architectural structure interprets space, and leads to hypotheses on the nature of space.'[27] Here at the start of Modern architecture can be found a seemingly intractable dichotomy between the theorist's disengaged and distant perspective and its insistence on the primacy of space, and the poet's intimately engaged and near-at-hand point of view and its revelation of the interdependence of space and construction. Though Modern architecture began with a space obsession, it has ironically devolved into today's object obsession, leaving behind the balanced composition of solid (wall) and void (room) that defines the making of inhabited interior space. The seemingly endless search for the new in much contemporary architectural design, theory and criticism has resulted in the profession largely losing touch with the dialogue between enclosed space and the tectonic which stands as the foundation of Modern architecture. Instead, architectural thinking today tends to overemphasize exterior form apprehended exclusively by vision, and this has almost inevitably come at the expense of constructed interior space, contextual anchorage in place and the experiential qualities of both.

In the work of the best contemporary practitioners, however, we find a remarkable synthesis of space and the tectonic of construction, achieved through their emphasis on the experience of the inhabitation of interior space. Separated and set in opposition in the theories that have scripted Modern architectural histories, space and the tectonic are rejoined, as fundamental complements, in the work of these contemporary practices. Their work indicates their understanding that the difference between architecture as exterior form and as interior space has to do with how it is experienced – at a distance from us or near to us. Like music, the space of a room, an interior, surrounds and encloses us, and can never be seen all at once – it does not stand in front of us as an object. In a lecture to architecture students, Aldo van Eyck, paraphrasing the painter Cézanne on nature, noted that the experience of architecture 'is on the inside. I do not see it according to its exterior envelope. I live in it from the inside. I am immersed in it. After all, the world is around me – not in front of me.'[28]

Sanctuary space and its structure reaching towards the natural light, floor articulated as a topography cascading down to riverside. Alvar Aalto, Church of the Assumption of Mary, Riola di Vergato, Italy, interior of sanctuary; sketch made on 2 October 1983.

Three

Three Early Modern Conceptions
of Interior Space

What have been recognized as the three most influential spatial 'discoveries' of early Modern architecture – still in use today and ordering contemporary works – all began with an inspiration about interior spatial experience. All three of these initiatory design conceptions are physically grounded in the floor plan. Frank Lloyd Wright's early work served to inspire the major later developments of what came to be known as Modern architecture, and in making these designs, he noted that the floor or ground plan, the topographic surface upon which inhabitants stand and move, was of pre-eminent importance. The floor plan came first and determined the development of the entire design. The building was conceived as being generated from the ground plan, and it gave form and order to the space within to be lived in. In 1908 Wright wrote that the floor plan was the interior spatial 'solution' and the elevation was the exterior formal 'expression' of an organic, integrated whole.[1] Wright believed that the floor plan – the plane upon which life takes place within the building – contained the core concept of the space within: 'Were all the elevations of the genuine buildings of the world lost and the ground plans saved, each building would reconstruct itself again.'[2] The ground plan shaped and formed the interior space, and the only reason to shape the space within was for the experience of the inhabitants.

The 'woven plan' that Wright developed in his early Prairie period, beginning in 1890 and evolving until his death in 1959, was the first of the three plan types to redefine and transform interior spatial experience at the beginning of Modern architecture.[3] As we have seen, the earliest examples of these remarkably innovative floor plans, and the interior spaces they formed, were built within houses whose exterior appearance gave no indication whatsoever of the dynamic spatial structure existing within. The 'woven plans' of Wright's Prairie houses, first fully realized on both interior and exterior in 1900 with the construction of the Hickox and Bradley Houses, were characterized by an unprecedented – and still largely unmatched – degree of both spatial freedom and formal order. Yet despite their seemingly infinite variety, the plans of the hundreds of Prairie houses Wright would design during this thirty-year period were all composed as variations on the themes of only two cruciform floor plan types – what he called the 'tripartite' plan and the 'pinwheel' plan – that he had evolved from the plan of his own Oak Park house of 1889.[4] In the tripartite plan two volumes interpenetrate to form a stable square space at the centre, while in the pinwheel plan four volumes rotate around and interlock at a solid centre.

Wright is famous, at least partly due to his own rhetoric, for his 'destruction of the box' used to define the traditional room, yet experience of the interiors of his houses indicates that such singular interpretations are misleading. Rather than destroying the enclosure afforded by the rectangular volume of the room, Wright increased both the precision and the ambiguity of spatial definition in his rooms. His work was not an attack on the idea of the room, but an enrichment of its experience. Wright destroyed the singular interpretation of the room as he re-engaged issues of space-making and inhabitation, grappling with the questions of how one defines a volume, a place and experience in space. As just one example, the cruciform plans of his houses provided light and views on three sides to all the major rooms on their ground floors – to this day an exceptional and largely unmatched condition in house design, but one that would be the norm for Wright's houses throughout his 72-year career.

In designing the interior spaces of his Prairie houses, Wright deployed proportions, geometry and modular grids to frame and shape the experience of the inhabitant; as John Dewey said of architecture: 'It is a matter of proportions qualitatively felt.'[5] Wright dramatically increased the complexity, ambiguity and richness of the spaces within his buildings, yet the geometric order with which these rooms were structured allowed the inhabitants to clearly perceive the interlocking and interpenetration of spaces in the house. This is illustrated by the photographs of Wright's houses taken for publication, wherein Wright positioned furniture to indicate the highly dynamic nature of the spaces, and placed rugs so they overlapped and ran across room divisions and through doorways to indicate the interweaving of spaces that result from the movement of occupants and the interpenetration of tradition-ally separate rooms.

Wright's system of design, while often labelled as abstract, was in fact measured by, scaled by and calibrated precisely to the human body and the experience of inhabitation; as Wright said, 'form became feeling.'[6] The interior spaces of Wright's build-ings appealed at a fundamental level to the occupant's sense of embodied presence and bodily movement, interpreted through experience. Wright conceived of the room as being composed of a series of horizontal layers of space, from the floor to the ceiling, with varying wall and beam heights between, which are carefully modulated to human scale, to the occupant's activity and the resulting position of the eye. When standing in a Wright house, one can see in all directions, and there appear to be only piers at the perimeter, with no walls in the traditional sense. Yet by sitting down, one finds oneself within the protective enclosure of low walls and built-in cabinetry, with views limited to the interior.

In Wright's interiors, the intellectual and formal order of the plan is balanced by the physical and spiritual engagement of the inhabitant; for Wright concept and experience were one and the same.

Wright stated that integrity was the most important principle at work in his designs. This integrative imperative is most evident in Wright's designs of rooms, which are defined by the complementary ordering concepts of independent architectural elements and spatial fusion. Wright defined architecture 'conceived as space enclosed' by separating and articulating the components of the room – floors, walls, ceilings, structure, windows, doors, stairs and furniture – and giving them independence as elements so that they might be utilized to structure space more precisely: 'Walls now apparent more as humanized screens. They do define and differentiate, but never confine and obliterate space.'[7] The walls, floors and ceilings, when deployed as independent elements, allowed Wright to simultaneously define spaces more precisely and fuse them into more ambiguous compositions. The complexly overlapping spatial volumes that resulted provided inhabitants with a richer and more varied set of experiences than was typical of other houses of the period.

The integral order resulting from Wright's combining elemental independence and spatial fusion was made constitutional in the floor plan. The primary ordering concept structuring Wright's 'woven plans' is the square grid, which he called the 'unit system'. The square grid in plan was essential both as a compositional method, employed to modulate interior space into wide and narrow bands, and as a way of ordering the construction, employed to locate and anchor structural and enclosure components to the floor. The grid may be understood as the warp and woof structuring the weaving of space. Wright employed the square grid to 'keep all to scale, ensure consistent proportion throughout the edifice, large or small, which thus became – like tapestry – a consistent woven fabric of independent related units, however various.'[8] Wright conceived of architecture as a weaving: 'All the buildings I have ever built are fabricated upon a unit system as the pile of a rug is stitched into the warp,'[9] and he said he considered himself 'a weaver', not a sculptor. He also used the terms 'textiles', 'textured' and 'fabrics' to describe his own buildings.[10]

In Wright's houses, the floor is a stable, continuous plane, while the ceiling is formed by multiple planes that are raised and lowered to respond to the specific activities that take place in each space – low at the fireplace and dining area, where people were seated, and high at the living room and stair, where people were standing or walking. This precision of definition resulted in the creation of multiple ceiling heights, each defining a different space, yet all within the single space defined by the floor plane. The floor plane, on which the inhabitants stand and walk, while of necessity more subtle in its movements than the ceiling above, is nevertheless the more powerful shaper of experience. Wright recognized that, owing to the natural fear of losing one's footing, people are more attentive to the floor than to the ceiling when they are moving through an interior – and this is even more evident when ascending and descending stairs. The interiors of Wright's houses were constructed of multiple spaces, formed by the contrapuntal axial and cross-axial directions of the volumes defined by the floors and the ceilings, which were woven together and held in tension. As a result, the experience of moving within the interior was defined not so much by bounding walls as by the syncopated spatial rhythm of compression and release formed between the more dynamic ceilings overhead and more stable floors underfoot as they overlapped and intersected one another.

The 'woven plan' involved the interpenetration of interior spaces organized through the layering of the floor and ceiling, rather than the screen-walls, and can be related to the East Asian concepts of the ground platform and the roof canopy.[11] Wright wrote of rooms as being both caves and tents, joining two dichotomous conceptions of the space within: a dark, earthbound, anchored and protected place of collective ritual, centred on the hearth, and a centrifugal expansion of space and view to the distant horizon in all directions, with its sense of freedom and individual independence. The floor and its bounding walls belong to the earth, and the roof belongs to the sky, forming the space within between: 'In the way the walls rose from the plan and the spaces were roofed over was the chief interest of the house.'[12] For Wright, the primary generator of 'the space within' was the ground plan: 'A good plan is the beginning and the end . . . its development in all directions is inherent – inevitable.'[13]

The Viennese architect Adolf Loos's concept of *Raumplan* (room plan), fully developed in his works from 1918 until his death in 1932, came next in this sequence of Modern generative conceptions of interior space. In Loos's 'room plans', each of the primary public rooms of the house (but not the private bedrooms) had its own appropriate proportions, light quality and material character, and its own position in plan and section, leading to plans that were fractured into multiple levels, forming a kind of domestic interior terrain or topography. Though Loos did not himself use the term *Raumplan* for his work, he did describe it as 'the solution of how to arrange the living rooms in three dimensions, not on the flat plane . . . For that is the great revolution in architecture: the three-dimensional rendering of the ground-plan!'[14]

Loos characterized his 'room plans' as primarily concerned with the making of rooms appropriate for their respective occupations, carefully positioned in space and precisely related to each other,

Working within the symmetrical structure of older buildings, new display elements organize the space as a series of localized and intimate experiences placed within an open modern plan. Carlo Scarpa, Museo Correr, Venice, Italy, detail of mounting of unframed paintings on easel (top), and Carlo Scarpa, Museo di Castelvecchio, Verona, Italy, plan of second sculpture gallery, with three raised sculpture bases faced in polished plaster (bottom); sketches made on 12 and 13 November 2013.

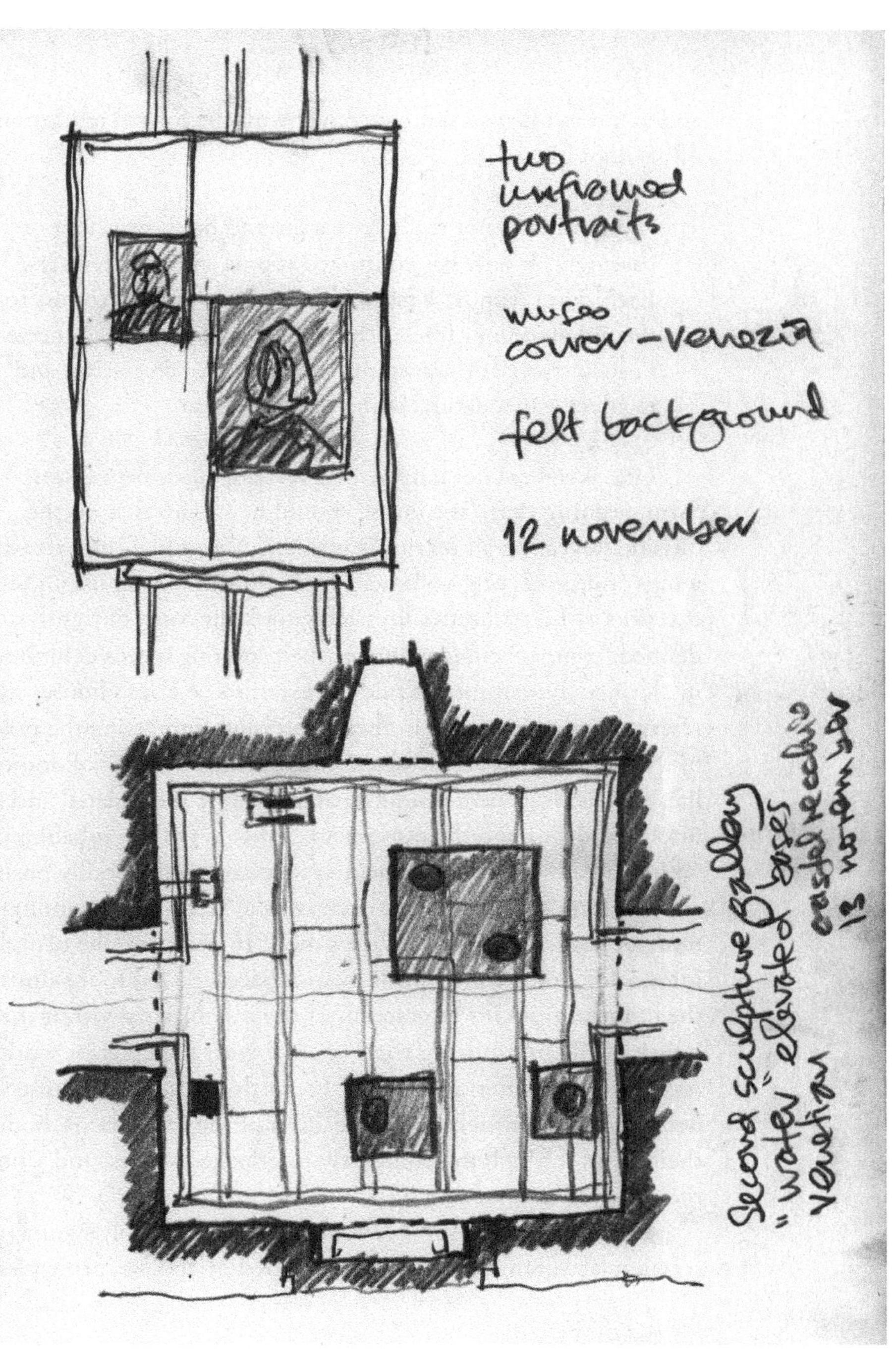

two
unframed
portraits

museo
correr - venezia

felt background

12 november

Second sculpture Gallery
"water" elevated bases
castal reactive
Venetian
13 november

and as a result he was not concerned with the formal resolution of his floor plans:

> My work does not really have a ground floor, first floor or basement. It only has connected rooms, annexes, terraces. Each room requires a particular height . . . that accounts for the different floor levels. The rooms must then be connected in such a way as to make the transition imperceptible, and to effect it in a natural and efficient fashion.[15]

Like Wright, Loos emphasized interior space over exterior form, arguing that 'The house should be withdrawn on the outside, revealing all its riches inside.'[16] Yet unlike the extending wings and projecting volumes of Wright's Prairie houses, the exteriors of Loos's houses invariably took the form of tightly defined, compact cubic volumes, their interior spaces delimited in all three dimensions. While the exteriors of Loos's houses were reserved and anonymous in their expression, protecting the privacy of the inhabitants, on the interior, the primary rooms of domestic life, each with its own unique character, were interrelated and interlocked through the movement and views of the inhabitants within the house. Loos was acutely sensitive to the bodily position and resulting eye levels of the occupants in section: 'One millimetre more or less in cross-section hurts me.'[17] In daily use, the complex interlocking of the interior domestic spaces tended to maximize the opportunities for interaction of the inhabitants within the house, while minimizing their contact with the exterior world. As a result, the interior spaces of Loos's domestic architecture were defined almost entirely by the position of the inhabitants' bodies, their views through the complexly interlocked spaces, and whom they were able to see and hear.

The primary rooms in Loos's houses were invariably symmetrical rectangular volumes, each at once centred on its own principle apertures and fixtures (such as the fireplace) while simultaneously being opened to the neighbouring rooms through the layering of walls and screens, overlapping volumes and shared stairs. The entrance to the house was on the closed street front, while the main living rooms were placed at the back, opening to the private garden. As a result, movement from the entry to the living room proceeded diagonally across the section, upwards and from front to back. While the interior rooms were rectangular and symmetrical, the movement sequence of stairs and landings was not placed on the central axis of the house, but was instead arranged to create a rotating, spiralling movement sequence similar to the rotating arrangement of the rooms to which the stairs led. Paralleling the rotational movement of the stair sequence was the primary movement along the edge of the rooms, rather than through their centres, allowing the centres of the rooms to be occupied by stable arrangements of furnishings.

In the 'room plan', the complex, almost labyrinthine movement sequences spiralled around, intertwined with and interlocked the various public rooms of the house, allowing the occupants views into and through rooms from multiple positions in the plan and section. The domestic realm was composed of a cluster of inter-penetrating, overlapping primary rooms, and Loos paid particular attention to the relation between the living room and the dining room, and to giving them contrasting experiential qualities. He invariably positioned the smaller, more intimate dining room precisely one metre above the living room, to which it opened, so that when seated at the dining table the family could still overlook the larger living room. From house to house, Loos would vary the contrasting qualities of the two primary rooms, either giving the smaller dining room the greater light by way of large apertures, while the larger living room onto which the dining room opened was shadowed, dark and introverted, or making a shadowed dining room overlook a more brightly lit living room. Yet in all of his 'room plans', by placing the stairs in the living room, or between the living room and dining room, Loos made the rooms both more spacious and more complexly layered and ambiguously bounded.

Loos criticized architects whose 'imaginations create not spaces but walls. That which is left over around the walls then forms the rooms,' going on to argue instead that 'the architect first senses the effect that he intends to realize and sees the rooms he wants to create in his mind's eye.'[18] The effect the room has on the inhabitants is produced by a combination of the qualities of the materials and the precise shape of the interior room. Loos varied materials from room to room to create the appropriate mood for the activity that would take place therein. The rich palette of wall veneer materials, from coloured marble to dark wood to woven fabrics, created a dense and intimate interior atmosphere within the houses. Instead of conceiving the house as originating from his own preconceived design ideas, Loos went so far as to say that he needed to see his client's favourite armchair in order to discern how the room in which it would sit was to be designed. Rather than designing the furniture for his clients, Loos insisted on his clients furnishing their houses to their own taste, increasing the interior's intimate, intensely personal feeling. Due to the embodied experience of interior space that he sought in his designs, Loos was against having his interiors photographed:

> For photography renders insubstantial, whereas what I want in my rooms is for people to feel substance around them, for it to act upon them, for them to know the enclosed space, to feel the fabric, the wood, above all to perceive it sensually, with sight and touch, for them to dare to sit comfortably . . .[19]

The Swiss-French architect and painter Le Corbusier's *plan libre* (free plan) is the third, and arguably most influential, of the three concepts of interior space as generative that emerged at the beginning of Modern architecture. The 'free plan', which evolved in Le Corbusier's work from 1922 onwards until his death in 1965, was the most important of his 'five points' developed as a critique of traditional architecture, in both its form and its construction of space, and as a formula for the production of Modern architecture. The 'five points' (in the order in which Le Corbusier introduced them in 1927) included the *pilotis* (columns), which lifted the building off the ground; the roof garden, which together with the *pilotis* allowed people to occupy spaces with nature and sunlight both below and above the building; the *plan libre*, made possible by the separation of the structural columns from the (now) non-load-bearing interior and exterior walls; the continuous horizontal window; and the *façade libre* (free facade), made possible by the recessing of the building structure from the outer walls to the interior. The pivotal element of the 'five points', and the point without which the others would not be possible, is the 'free plan', which Le Corbusier introduced third in the sequence – at the centre of the 'five points' – with the bottom and top of the building preceding, and the facades following.

The 'free plan' was primarily dependent upon Le Corbusier's conception of the construction prototype he called the Maison Dom-ino, which he developed between 1915 and 1919. The volume was formed by stacked rectangular floor slabs, into the thickness of which all spanning structure was embedded, which were supported by columns that were inset from the long sides of the rectangular form. The resulting interior spaces had no load-bearing walls and no exposed horizontal ceiling structure (such as beams), allowing for the positioning of the space-shaping interior walls of the 'free plan', and the arrangement of the continuous horizontal windows and other apertures on the 'free facades', to be unconstrained by vertical or horizontal structure. The rectangular forms of the houses Le Corbusier designed using the 'five points' and the 'free plan' were carefully chosen by the architect, and it is not coincidental that both the plans and the facades of Le Corbusier's early houses are often organized as rectangles based on squares and Golden Sections (1:1.618 ratio), exemplary of the 'proportional regulation of surfaces' that determined the two most typical canvas shapes he deployed in his Purist paintings of the period.

Le Corbusier's Purist paintings were almost exclusively still-lifes, and the objects he depicted were most often hollow volumes, vessels, containers, bottles, vases, glasses and guitars. These hollow volumes were presented in vertical axonometric projection, seen in both plan (from above) and elevation (from in front), and their straight and curving profiles matched those of neighbouring volumes in the composition. Le Corbusier called this primacy of profiles the 'marriage of contours', and he applied it to both his painting and the interior spaces of his architecture. 'The marriage of contours' referred to the sharing or echoing of profiles that allows objects or spaces to mesh together like the gears in a machine – one line/wall could serve as the edge of more than one object/space. The 'marriage of contours' in Le Corbusier's 'free plans' allowed an overlapping, intersecting, integrating and layering of interior spaces, wherein the wall was developed as the profile or contour shared by two or more spaces.

In Le Corbusier's 'free plan', the floor plane is occupied by straight, angled and curving walls, all freely disposed to shape the space of inhabitation and the movement path through the plan, limited only by the perimeters of the rectangular floor plans and building volumes. Le Corbusier described the experience of walking through the interior spaces formed by the walls of the 'free plan' as the *promenade architecturale*, wherein the concave curve creates an 'interior' surrounded by the convex curved 'exterior', only to reverse a few steps later in the movement sequence. This sharing of profiles or contours allows a figure-ground fluctuation of spatial interpretations; in the 'free plan', 'inside/concave' and 'outside/convex' are no longer set, and a reversal occurs as we walk from one 'inside' to another 'inside' during our *promenade architecturale*. The 'free plan' allowed Le Corbusier to construct interiors characterized by spatial ambiguity, with reversed readings and multiple spatial interpretations suggesting multiple spatial viewpoints, which are experienced in walking through the spaces of a building. In a similar way to Wright's 'woven plan', Le Corbusier's 'free plan' and its 'marriage of contours', while employing pure geometric volumes, increases both the precision of the spaces and the multiple spatial interpretations they inspire in inhabitation.

The 'free plan' and the *promenade architecturale* it shapes are essentially about interior space, ordered by the experience of the inhabitant as they move through the carefully orchestrated sequence of unfurling interior volumes. For Le Corbusier, the 'free' floor plan, like the surface of a Purist canvas on which the profiles/walls were to be arranged, was of paramount importance, and as a result the section was far less developed, articulated and active in shaping the experience of interior space in all his early buildings. The topographic character of the floor planes of the 'free plan' was likely also related to Le Corbusier's contemporary study of the work of the theatrical designer Adolphe Appia, who defined architecture as the grouping of anchored masses into 'rhythmic spaces', rectangular 'terrains' revealed by light and shadow, which were arranged and 'measured according to the scale of the living body, and intended for the movement of that body'.[20] In defining the function of windows, Le Corbusier privileged the floor plane over the wall plane, into which the window is opened, by writing: 'my architecture is lighted floors.'[21] The resulting dominance of the (vertical) interior walls by the dictates of the (horizontal) 'free plan' floor is suggested by Kenneth Frampton's description of the *promenade architecturale* through Le Corbusier's Villa Savoye of 1929 as 'a topographic itinerary in which the floor planes, bent upwards to form ramps and stairs, are fused with the walls so as to create the illusion that the subject is literally "walking up the walls"'.[22]

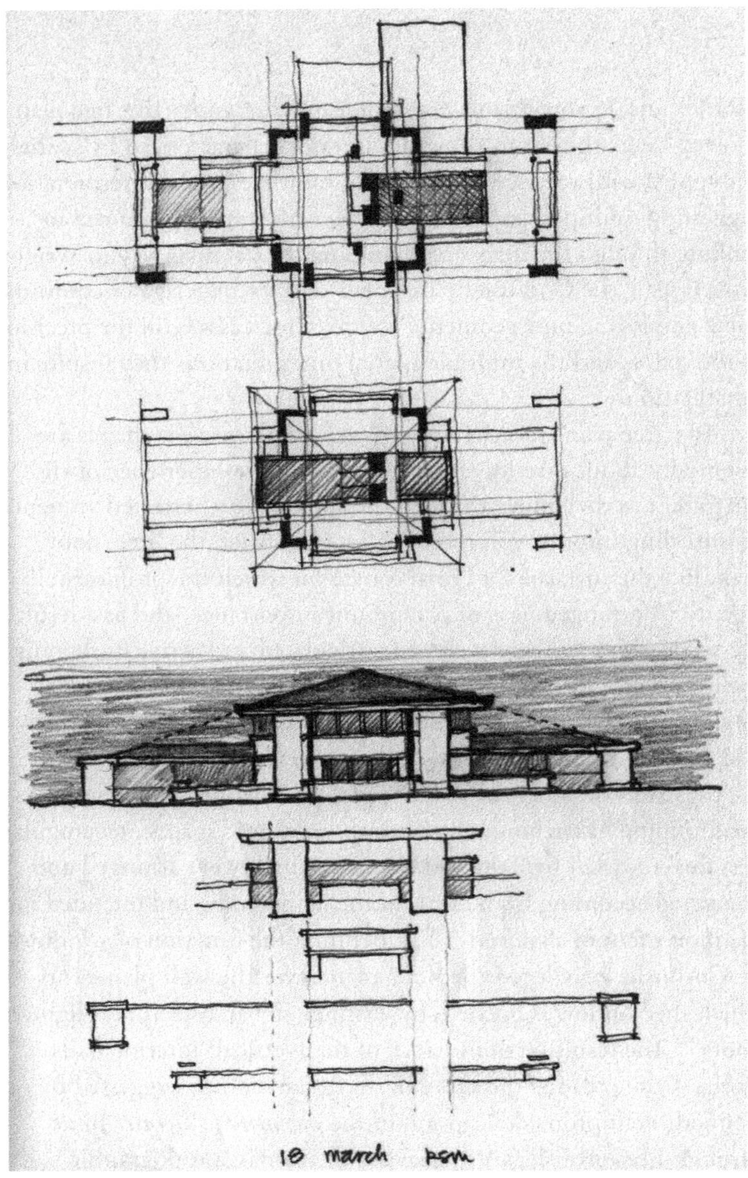

Approached from outside, the symmetrical house has a closed centre, and entry is achieved by moving along outer edges of walled volumes, passing through thresholds formed by roof overhangs, and moving along inner edges before arriving in the central living room. Frank Lloyd Wright, Evans House, Chicago, Illinois, analysis of plan and elevation; sketch made on 18 March 1986.

Four

The Separate Paths of the Eye and the Body in Experience

A shared characteristic of the majority of spatial concepts developed in early Modern architecture, including the De Stijl designs of Gerrit Rietveld, the early pinwheel plans of Ludwig Mies van der Rohe, as well as the three conceptions of how to order interior space of Wright, Loos and Le Corbusier examined in the last chapter, is that they were all developed in opposition to the manner of designing buildings promulgated by the École des Beaux-Arts in Paris – the dominant design method in the nineteenth century and the first quarter of the twentieth century in Europe and the Americas. The vast majority of buildings designed by École des Beaux-Arts-trained architects, irrespective of function and location, were organized using strict axial planning and bilateral symmetry. In experience, the eye of the inhabitant was able to look down the central axis on which their body would eventually move to reach the axially aligned goal, so that the paths of the eye and the body, in following the movement route to the destination, were exactly the same. Yet, as we have noted earlier, when the eye and the body are equally engaged in the inhabitation of architecture, the eye and the visual sense invariably dominates the experience, overpowering the other, subtler senses, including the synthetic, haptic sense of bodily position in space.

In counterpoint to this visual-centric approach, early Modern buildings shared the characteristic that the path of the inhabitant's eye was almost never the same as the path of their body. Rather than seeing and moving along the same central axis through the same sequence of spaces, the inhabitant meandered in plan and section through the interior spaces of the building. While the inhabitant may have been able to see directly to the goal or destination, their body was unable to physically navigate that route, and they were encouraged to find a different path, taking their eye off the goal and thus becoming aware of other internal vistas as well as perceiving multiple viewpoints of the same interior spaces. Yet this separation of the paths of the eye and body in the experience of interior spaces in early Modern architecture was often accomplished using symmetry and axial planning – the same ordering principles of ancient architecture that had been stultified into academic formulas by the École des Beaux-Arts. It was the manner in which architects such as Wright, Loos and Le Corbusier engaged these classical architectural ordering principles that made such a profound difference in the resulting experience of the space within.

The modern transformation of 'the space within' begins with Wright, who argued that symmetry and axial planning were a basic component of human space making throughout historical time, and that such ordering ideas therefore could not belong to any one time, school or style of architecture. In the 1914 edition of his essay series *In the Cause of Architecture*, Wright noted how at the beginning of his career as an architect he 'deliberately chose to break with traditions [the formulaic and derivative designs of the Beaux-Arts-trained academic classicists] in order to be more true to Tradition [the great architecture of history] than current conventions and ideals in architecture would permit'. Making clear that he was denying the formula of 'traditional' academic designs, while simultaneously reclaiming from the École des Beaux-Arts the fundamental ordering principles to be found in the great architectural precedents of history, Wright also rejected the anti-classical slogan of his younger contemporaries – 'progress before precedent' – as an 'unthinking, unthinkable thing'.[1]

Wright's early Prairie period buildings are almost invariably symmetrical in massing, pyramidal or cubic in exterior form, and their floor plans are often bi-axially symmetrical, with the volumes aligning along the axis and cross-axis that meet at the solid hearth (in the houses) or the void of the main space (in the public buildings). Yet, while Wright employed what he called 'a simple axial law and order' in designing his buildings, he also allowed that, 'although the symmetry may not be obvious, always the balance is maintained.'[2] When standing in front of a Wright building, the symmetrical massing clearly indicates the destination of the main room within, yet the central volume (and its central ordering axis) is solid, blocked to both entry and movement. As a result, entry to Wright's buildings is anything but 'obvious' and, confronted with the symmetrical, axial, closed exterior form, the person wishing to enter searches for a way in. Entry is gained only after walking along a spiralling movement sequence that, rather than proceeding directly to the centre of the building, involves moving around the edges of the exterior volumes to discover the secluded entrance door.

Once inside the building, the spiralling entry sequence continues as one moves along the edges of spaces, entering each succeeding room at its corner rather than at its centre, until, after executing a number of right-angled turns, one arrives at the destination, the living room or main space, always aligned with the central axis of the floor plan. The rediscovery and occupation of the central volume first seen from the exterior only occurs after passing through an intentionally obscured entry sequence, and access to the space within requires a conscious effort on the part of the inhabitant to decipher the underlying order of the design. In finally arriving in the primary interior space, there is a sense that no goal or destination is worth attaining without effort, and the desirability of the destination increases with each new barrier to reaching it.

Wright utilized axial symmetry in a way that made entry and movement through the interior spaces of his buildings more complex and ambiguous than was to be expected, given their seemingly simple exterior forms. He intentionally lengthened the path, increased the number of different angles from which the building and its spaces were seen, and varied the space, material and natural light along the entry path in contrast to those characterizing the final goal – a dark, compressed, circuitous, peripheral route leading to a bright, expansive central space. In Wright's public buildings, the goal of the movement route is the main room, while in his houses the sequence of movement arrives at several successive destinations – the entry hall, living room and finally dining room. From each room, the next room is often visible through a wood slat screen, but one must execute a right-angled turn of both the eye and the body to enter it. In allowing inhabitants to move only along the edges of spaces and to enter rooms at their corners, rather than at their centres, Wright's house interiors are initially perceived as an unfolding series of dynamic, centrifugal diagonal views across interlocking rectangular rooms. Yet, upon arriving in the centre of each room, it is perceived as being centripetally anchored at its ends by symmetrical solid hearths and window walls that face each other along the room's central axis. In all his buildings, Wright designed the movement sequence of the occupant to be a counterpoint to the pure geometries, modular grid and axial symmetry of his floor plans. For Wright, the inhabitant's position was as important as the spatial composition in determining the experience of his architecture.

The fundamentally haptic, multi-sensorial and embodied experience of Wright's interior spaces had a profound influence on modern architects, as is indicated by the American architect Marcel Breuer's statement:

What I value most of [Wright's] achievements is his sense of interior space. It is a liberated space – to be experienced not only by your eye, but felt by your touch: dimensions and modulations corresponding to your steps and movements.[3]

Breuer believed that architecture was 'the art of space', and his description of an ideal interior space, and the nature of its experience, are directly related to both Wright's buildings and his concept of 'the space within':

> The nature of the space within our buildings and between them is indeed the reality of architecture . . . The exact rhythm of space-successions is the art of architecture. It cannot be defined by hard and fast rules – though there are some simple and successful formulas: emerging from a narrow, darker, low-ceilinged space into a light, high, large space is an exciting experience . . . The eye is the only receiving instrument in the experience of painting. But we have seen that the experience of architecture is received by the whole body, by all our senses . . . It is not only an eye aesthetic, it is a *physical aesthetic*.[4]

The house designs of Adolf Loos were founded on the primacy of interior space, and the construction of a private domestic world within, concealed from the public world of the city street. Loos's houses all presented rigorously axially symmetrical facades to the street, with central entryways and paired windows often suggesting mask-like facial features. Yet, once inside, the entry axis was blocked and the inhabitants were invited to execute a series of right-angled turns up short flights of stairs with numerous landings. Drawn upwards by the natural light, one ascended in a labyrinthine, repeatedly turning movement sequence up to the main floor of the house, with its subtly stepped topography. After arriving in the living room, the largest and tallest of the primary domestic spaces, one became aware of several other spaces opening off the living room, their floors set at a higher level. The dining room, its floor elevated one metre above the living room, was opened to the living room along an entire wall. The two rooms, provided with contrasting light and views, often together created a theatrical character, with the smaller and higher dining room as the stage and the larger and lower living room as the seating. Small, intimate rooms protected by screen walls were often positioned adjacent to the large open living room, allowing inhabitants to look into the living room and listen in on conversations without being seen. The complex labyrinthine intertwining of rooms, floor levels, openings, stairs and landings created a series of carefully calibrated vantage points within the main rooms, from which the inhabitant was able, by moving only a few steps, to gain an entirely different view from one room into the next.

Le Corbusier's polemic against the dominance of the École des Beaux-Arts was even more virulent than Wright's, no doubt due to his proximity to the source. Le Corbusier's 1923 book *Vers une architecture* was a sustained argument for the ancient principles of architectural order to be re-engaged in new works not tied to the dominant Beaux-Arts design methods. He diagrammed the proportional 'regulating lines' structuring the facades of historical monuments, such as Notre-Dame de Paris and Michelangelo's Campidoglio in Rome, and presented the 'lessons of Rome' to be found in the interior spaces of the Pantheon and Santa Maria in Cosmedin. Even more explicitly than Wright, Le Corbusier argued that axial symmetry and proportional systems belonged to architecture as a discipline, and not to any stylistic school or academic approach. His first example of the use of 'regulating lines' was 'a primitive temple', a large tent enclosed in a walled precinct and ordered using a double square in plan, about which he stated:

It is the plan of a house, or the plan of a temple. It is the same spirit one finds again in the Pompeian house. It is the spirit

Symmetrically organized interior volumes blocked along central axes and opening at corners to adjacent spaces, with the movement of the occupants structured in a spiral around the central gallery. Brad Cloepfil, Clyfford Still Museum, Denver, Colorado, interior view of open corner of central gallery (top), and diagram of the relation of the central gallery in plan to lateral galleries and in section to vertical voids (below); sketch made on 16 November 2011.

central gallery open to two
lateral galleries, two vertical
spaces

plan

section

16 november

plan

indeed of the Temple of Luxor. There is no such thing as primitive man; there are primitive resources. The idea is constant, in full sway from the beginning.[5]

In a similar way to both Wright and Loos, Le Corbusier's early houses almost invariably had symmetrical front facades, and the columns that structure their floor plans were often organized on syncopated grids, alternating wide and narrow bays – a characteristic shared with the domestic plans of Andrea Palladio, as Colin Rowe has shown.[6] Entry was usually in the narrow bay to the left or right of the blocked wide bay at the centre, but once inside, the inhabitants found that the balanced symmetrical disposition of the facade bore no relation to the dynamic space unfurling around them. Rather than having their movement shaped by curving and angled walls, the inhabitants were presented with the plastic concave and convex forms of freestanding staircases and ramps, and openings in the ceilings overhead set diagonally across the space. Between the front door and the final destination – often an exterior terrace open to the sky and the landscape, rather than the living or dining room – the inhabitants were led along the meandering path of the *promenade architecturale*, crossing and re-crossing the central axis of symmetry in a series of diagonal movements, culminating in a dynamically asymmetrical and almost entirely open rear facade of the house. At almost every point along the way, the view given to the eye and the path required of the body varied dramatically, often going in different directions, resulting in a richly textured and deeply layered experience.

In this case of the similarity or difference in the spatial itineraries of the eye and the body, the exceptions prove the rule. While the vast majority of buildings designed in accordance with the academic methods of the École des Beaux-Arts are characterized by the paths of the eye and the body both being subjected to the same linear movement along the building's central axis, a few of the very best buildings of the era have different paths for eye and body, and are thus closer in the way they are inhabited to contemporary Modern buildings. A prime example would be the New York Public Library, completed in 1911 to the designs of the École des Beaux-Arts-trained Carrère & Hastings, where after climbing up the monumental staircase (its cascading form a subtle reminder of the city reservoir that previously occupied the urban site) and entering on axis through the central door and into the central entry hall, one finds the axial centre across the entry hall blocked to bodily movement, while the destination is seen to be ahead and above, at the top of the entry hall. One must then choose to ascend either the staircase on the right or that on the left, and the movement sequence only comes back to the axial centre of the plan at the very top of the building, where one finds oneself in the main reading room situated above the six floors of book stacks, the height of which one just measured in the ascension of the stairs.

In parallel to the concept of a rich interlacing of the visual and physical movement paths through interior space, the philosopher Henri Bergson, a contemporary of the early Modern architects, began his *Time and Free Will* of 1889 with the statement:

> We necessarily express ourselves by means of words and we usually think in terms of space. That is to say, language requires us to establish between our ideas the same sharp and precise distinctions, the same discontinuity, as between material objects.[7]

Bergson argued that human experience was dominated by the internal and intensive, concentrated conditions that resulted in time being experienced as enduring and continuous, and space as both compressed and released into its bounds. On the other hand, experience was diminished by the external and extensive, dispersed conditions that resulted in time being experienced as divided and discontinuous, and space as both quantified and undifferentiated. Bergson noted our propensity for

> intermingling of the purely intensive sensation of mobility with
> the extensive representation of the space traversed. On the one
> hand we attribute to the motion the divisibility of the space
> which it traverses, forgetting that it is quite possible to divide
> an *object*, but not an *act*: and on the other hand we accustom
> ourselves to projecting this act itself into space, to applying it
> to the whole of the line which the moving body traverses, in
> a word, to solidifying it.

Instead of the extensive understanding of fixed time and divided space, Bergson believed the intensive experience in flowing time was 'a process of unfolding in space'.[8]

The separate paths of the eye and the body in the experience of interior space, as they were developed in early Modern architecture, have also been related to the psychological concept of 'prospect and refuge' developed by Jay Appleton in his book *The Experience of Landscape*.[9] Appleton argues that in order to comfortably inhabit the landscape (or a building) it is necessary for us to be able to see without being seen; to have 'prospect' – to be able to see outwards in many directions, and to see anyone approaching our position from the exterior, while ourselves remaining secluded and protected within a 'refuge' – a sheltered space where we cannot be seen by anyone outside. In his book *The Wright Space*, Grant Hildebrand has shown how the houses of Wright, with their continuous bands of windows withdrawn behind the heavy protective masonry masses and recessed beneath the low overhanging roofs, allowing those within the deeply shadowed interior spaces to see out to the brightly lit exterior spaces without themselves being seen, are exemplary of places that provide their inhabitants both prospect and refuge.[10] The architectural historian Vincent Scully engaged the embodied interior experiential meaning of prospect and refuge (while simultaneously alluding to a contemporary film title, *A Room with a View*) when he described a Wright house as 'a womb with a view'.[11] For Wright, the exterior prospect from the interior refuge of the sheltered room also embodied the view to the horizon, indicative for Wright of human freedom:

> An idea (probably rooted deep in instinct) that shelter should be the essential look of any dwelling . . . I began to see the building primarily not as a cave but as broad shelter in the open, related vista; vista without and vista within.[12]

Related to the concept of the separate paths of the eye and the body, the philosopher and poet Paul Valéry, a contemporary of Le Corbusier and an admirer of the architect's early works, remarked on the essential nature of the experience of the body enclosed in space in his 1921 dialogue *Eupalinos; or, The Architect*. In it, the architect starts by stating:

> When I design a dwelling . . . I confess, however strange it may appear to you, *that it seems to me my body is playing its part in the game* . . . [It is through their body that people] participate in what they see and what they touch . . . They touch, they are touched.

Eupalinos goes on to note: 'the interior of this temple, forms for us a sort of complete greatness within which we live . . . We are, we move, we live inside.'[13]

In his remarkable essay of 1894, 'Introduction to the Method of Leonardo da Vinci', Valéry noted the tendency of disembodied, visual concepts to dominate sensual, embodied experiences:

> Most people see with their intellects more often than with their eyes. Instead of colored spaces, they become aware of concepts. Something whitish, cubical, erect, its planes broken by the sparkle of glass, is immediately a house for them – the House! – a complex idea, a combination of abstract qualities. If they change position, the movement of the rows of windows, the translation of surfaces

which continuously alters their sensuous perceptions, all this escapes them, for their concept remains the same. They perceive with a dictionary rather than with the retina; and they approach objects so blindly, they have such a vague notion of the difficulties and pleasures of vision, that they have invented *beautiful views*. Of the rest they are unaware.[14]

In conclusion, even a brief review of the concepts of interior space and its perception that were shared by early Modern architects and artists, as well as their shared critiques of the Neo-Classical interpretation of space and its fixed, singular point of view, serves to remind us that, at its beginnings some one hundred years ago, the Modern conception of space was understood by its exponents to include, integrate and engage all the arts. Primary among these parallels with art is the experience of multiple viewpoints within Modern buildings, produced by the inhabitant's eye being disengaged from the central axis of symmetry and invited, along with their body, to meander in plan and section through the interior spaces of the building. As has been noted, the early buildings of Wright, Loos and Le Corbusier were often characterized by symmetrical front facades, complemented and contrasted by the asymmetrical and meandering internal movement sequence, which allowed the inhabitant multiple viewpoints of the same spaces. This was paralleled in contemporary Cubist painting, where varied viewpoints are presented simultaneously in the single canvas. The critic John Berger observed that the capacity of Cubist paintings to hold multiple viewpoints of the same object and space within its spatial field was made possible by the way the Cubists 'created a continuity of structure [so that] space is part of the continuity of the events within it . . . The space between objects is part of the same structure as the objects themselves.'[15]

Other parallels between modern art and architecture include the intention to 'break the (exterior) box' that characterized both Wright's early work as well as the De Stijl architectonic designs of Gerrit Rietveld and Theo van Doesburg. In order to open the closed rectangular volume of traditional architecture, Wright and van Doesburg both projected space from a central core – a solid masonry hearth in the case of Wright, and the cubic void at the centre of the x–y–z axes in the case of the van Doesburg – with planar surfaces exfoliating outwards to form overlapping, interlocking peripheral edges. Another parallel is the conception of the space within and the planar surfaces that shape it being folded and unfolded, allowing both inside–outside reversals as well as constructing re-entrant corners, as evidenced in both the Prairie and Usonian houses of Wright and the artistic constructions of Paul Klee and Josef Albers. The experience of moving through interior spaces shaped by folded walls is suggested in Albers's description of his *Structural Constellations* as being 'in motion: from coming to going, in extension: from inward to outward, in grouping: from together to separated, in volume: from full to empty'.[16] Perhaps the most extended and productive sharing of principles between early Modern art and architecture was the unfurling of interior spaces in Le Corbusier's early works, which were made possible by the Purist painting-inspired 'marriage of contours'. As the architectural historian Colin Rowe and the painter Robert Slutzky have noted, the fluctuating inside–outside reversals occurring during the interior spatial experience of the *promenade architecturale* were characterized by 'simultaneity, interpenetration, superimposition, ambiguity . . . transparency'.[17]

Interior space defined by introduction of natural light, which is experienced as eroding the outer walls, illuminating the inner structure and carving the vaults of the ceiling. Alvar Aalto, Lakeuden Risti Church, Seinäjoki, Finland, interior double wall of window openings, structure and ceiling; sketch made on 15 September 2003.

Five

The Shape of Interior Space and the Boundary of Place

The tradition of architecture defined as interior space, going back to ancient times and extending through contemporary works, is one where the building may be said to be conceived not as an exterior form, but as an outer surface of interior space – the interior 'skin' of the inhabited room – in which the building allows the interior place of experience and inhabitation to unfold within the limits and boundaries set by the outer forms. This 'inside-out' reading of architecture – one determined by the outer boundary, surface and shape of the interior space – was best summarized by the second-generation Modern architect Aldo van Eyck in his 1958 appreciation of the interior-oriented architecture of Gerrit Rietveld, a founder of De Stijl:

[Rietveld] was one of the few to create space not so much by material boundaries but by the shaping of light . . . Rietveld is at his strongest when he is concerned with a single, separate space, whether or not its form is complex. Here the *periphery* of space constitutes the *matter* of its envelopment . . . Rietveld approaches the tangible, that which he must 'draw' and 'construct,' by way of the intangible, by way of light and space . . . he succeeds in approaching the material with which he has to build from the viewpoint of space; and not, as is usual, the other way round.[1]

The emphasis of early Modern architects on the shaping of the inner skin that defined inhabited space, as experienced from the interior, was at least partly inspired by the French engineer and art historian Auguste Choisy's books, including his *L'Art de bâtir chez les Romains* of 1873, illustrated with remarkably detailed axonometric interior views of the brick and concrete structural masses of the walls and vaulted ceilings of Roman architecture, and his monumental two-volume *Histoire de l'architecture* of 1899, a remarkably comprehensive study of architecture and construction from around the world and throughout history. The *Histoire* was the most important book of architectural history in the education of several generations of Modern architects, including Mies van der Rohe, Le Corbusier (who reproduced a number of Choisy's illustrations in his *Vers une architecture*), Alvar Aalto and Louis Kahn (who used Choisy's unique drawing techniques in illustrating his own designs).

The majority of the 1,760 line-drawing figures in Choisy's *Histoire* are what are called 'up-view' axonometrics, cut away in both plan and section and looking upwards – as if the walls of the buildings had been cut at the floor and lifted upwards, so that we are looking into the spaces from below the ground plane (leading to these drawings being called 'worm's-eye views', as opposed to 'bird's-eye views', seen from above). The half-floor plan is rendered in black, the full section is rendered in hatched gray, and profiles and corners of the walls and ceilings are rendered as single lines. The drawings, while depicting an astonishing range of architecture from around the world and across time, nevertheless present the diverse buildings as having a certain unity, through the shared drawing technique that emphasizes enveloping wall mass but not the specific material of construction, and above all by emphasizing the shaped volume of interior space. These influential drawings show almost nothing of the exterior of the buildings they depict, and instead strongly emphasize the interior surfaces of the walls and ceilings, and the way they are joined to shape and define the interior space in the great works of historical architecture in all eras.[2]

One of the most remarkable Modern analyses of both the perception and conception of inhabited space from the inside was made in 1952 by the Italian architect Luigi Moretti in his essay 'Structures and Sequences of Spaces'. He argued that, despite the tension created among and between the constituent elements of architecture such as '*chiaroscura*, constructive fabric, plasticity . . . density and quality of the materials, geometrical relations of the surfaces', all of which act to enclose interior space,

> there is, however, one expressive aspect that summarizes the architectural fact with such notable latitude that it seems it could be taken with greater tranquility than the others, even in isolation: I mean the internal and empty space.

The fact that interior space was the originating idea of architecture and the primary reason for constructing buildings 'was very clear to the ancients; for centuries . . . the conquests and resolution of internal spaces coincides with the very history of architecture itself'.[3]

Moretti illustrated his essay with a series of plaster models of the interior spaces of selected historical buildings, solidifying the inhabited interior voids while removing the containing mass of the outer walls (as if they were formwork for casting). In this way he quite literally gave plastic sculptural shape to what is enclosed within the building fabric, and to emphasize this transposition of void into solid, he called his analysis of interior space an 'internal stereometry', employing the term generally used to describe the three-dimensional curving geometry employed in the shaping of solid stones. Moretti identified the shared qualities of the 'sequences of internal volumes' in the analysed buildings: dimension (quantity of absolute volume); density (related to quantity and distribution of light); and pressure (related to the proximity of the bounding surfaces or masses), which acts to compress and release the flow of space.

Moretti begins his analysis with the Roman Hadrian's Villa, a prime example of 'the great spaces of architecture [that] arise with Rome'. The composition of pure geometrically shaped voids – rectangles, cubes, cylinders and spheres – connected by passageways carved in the thickness of the solid surrounding walls, serves as a (possibly intended) contrast to Le Corbusier's illustration in *Vers une architecture* at the end of his chapter 'The Lessons of Rome', where the outer forms of Roman buildings are juxtaposed to the primary geometric solids of which they are composed, both viewed from the exterior. Moretti followed with analyses of buildings by the Renaissance architects Andrea Palladio and Michelangelo, which were composed of clusters of carefully proportioned geometric volumes. He noted that Renaissance domestic interiors, such as the Palazzo Ducale at Urbino, were often composed of spatial 'sequences sculpted with extreme subtlety by differences of dimension alone, among volumes which maintain similar or identical geometrical forms.' The high point of Moretti's analysis of interior space involved a series of designs for church buildings by the late Baroque architect Guarino Guarini, in which he found 'the most precise concatenation of the volumes, the minor scansion of the passages, [and] the effulgence and attenuation of light as a distension and unfurling or unfolding of the spaces'.[4]

Yet despite the writings of critics from Schmarsow to Zevi that present the purported primacy of space in modern architectural design, Moretti argued that, with the exception of an unbuilt house project by Wright involving two interlocked cylinders, 'It seems the moderns have forgotten the laws of the sequence of interior volumes. They must conquer space as a sensitive, live element, and not by faithful extrapolation of graphic symbols.' Moretti maintained that the ways in which interior spaces were conceived and envisioned were of critical importance:

The errors modern architecture has committed through ignoring spaces in their concreteness can be judged in truth; [this] naturally assuming that modern architecture will live on truth, and has not been transferred as a cultural fact into its two-dimensional symbols, drawing and photography.[5]

It can be argued, however, that Moretti's volumetric casting method, and the elementary geometric figural conception of space that his castings present so admirably, were fundamentally unsuited to analysing the more ambiguously bounded spaces of much Modern architecture, including that of Wright. This is exemplified by Moretti's critique of Mies van der Rohe, whose work he argued involved the 'disassociation of a unitary space by means of screens and diaphragms'. In his analysis of the Villa Tugendhat in Brno (1930), Moretti argued that Mies,

> starting from a constructive volume of irregular geometric profile, disassociated space from it, preventing its integral and direct reading . . . by inserting into it screen walls and diaphragms that come to evoke unpredictable, uncertain boundary sectors.[6]

Yet the interweaving and layering of outer screen walls of varying heights, the interpenetration and overlapping of internal volumes, and the resulting experiential ambiguity of peripheral boundaries are in fact three of the primary characteristics of interior spaces in Modern architecture.

More recently, Moretti's plaster models of interior spaces, which turn inhabited void into sculptural solid in order that we may perceive it more precisely, has been complemented and contrasted by the drawings of the architect and educator Peter Magyar in his book *Spaceprints: A Handbook of Applied Topology in Architecture* (1984).[7] Magyar draws only the thin, skin-like outer surfaces of the walls that envelop and enclose interior space, and in this he quite literally demonstrates Van Eyck's idea that 'the *periphery* of space constitutes the *matter* of its envelopment.' Magyar's 'hollow' drawings are fundamentally concerned with space shaped for human habitation, and he argues: 'Space is perceptible for man only through "boundary conditions",' and that by way of drawings 'the exploration, articulation and evaluation of both container and contained can be simultaneously accomplished.'[8] Magyar understands this type of analytical drawing as a way of sensing precisely the spatial skins enclosing the rooms in which we live. When deployed in the synthetic process of designing, this type of drawing involves the active touching and shaping of the space of inhabitation, much as a potter shapes the clay to form the inner wall of a vessel. Magyar's drawings illustrate the fact that the void of interior space is perceptible only through the solid, constructed boundaries that enclose it – the internal surfaces that shape our interior experience.

In contrast to Moretti's analyses of historical examples of spatial enclosure, the Dutch monk and architect Dom Hans van der Laan took an anthropological approach to the definition of inhabited space in his 1983 book *Architectonic Space*. He defined the space formed by humans when building – which he called 'experience-space' – from the beginning: 'As a historian Choisy goes back to the stone age; the architect must go back to the foundations of architecture, which amounts to the same thing.' Van der Laan began by stating that the house is among the first things humans need to make in order to exist in nature, and in this effort he finds that the space-defining wall is primary. In his analysis, the limited mass of the walls is drawn up from the unlimited mass of the earth in order to demarcate a limited space of experience from the unlimited space of nature. As a result, the unlimited solid and void of earth below and atmosphere above, which are vertically related, is contrasted by the limited solid (walls) and void (experience-space) of architecture, which are horizontally related. Van der Laan drew his primary distinction between inside (inhabited) and outside (natural) space:

Layered outer walls of the sanctuary are filled with light, so that exterior space is experienced as pushing into the interior. Juha Leiviskä, Myyrmäki Church, Helsinki, Finland, interior view of clerestory light at wall and ceiling juncture; sketch made on 26 July 2006.

> Architectonic space [outside] owes its definition to the mass of the
> wall, which bounds the space from *without*. By contrast the space
> that we experience [inside] and relate to ourselves gets its definition
> from the activities of our various faculties, which determine its
> boundaries from *within*.
>
> The first space presents itself as a 'shell-space', since its
> limitation comes about from the external shell of solid walls,
> whereas the second space presents itself as a 'core-space', since its
> limitation is determined outwards from the core by means of our
> presence . . . The space-image of experience-space in the midst
> of natural space lends itself to the idea of fullness surrounded
> by emptiness, since experience-space is itself determined from
> within by our bodily presence.[9]

What Van der Laan called 'architectonic space . . . formed from
without by walls' involves an emptiness surrounded by the fullness
of natural space, while 'experience-space is itself determined from
within by our bodily presence', and involves a fullness surrounded
by the emptiness of natural space. The inside–outside relationship
is complemented by the solid–void relationship, where

> the void, the form of the space, is wholly dependent on the solid,
> the form of the mass. Space gets its form and hence its visibility
> from its involvement with the form of the wall . . . Walls are
> made, interior space comes into being.

In contrast to Moretti, Van der Laan gives primacy to the
'active' mass-walls over the 'passive' interior space: 'we form the
walls, and from them the inside space that comes into being
between them must borrow its form.' Interior spatial volume
is bounded by surfaces, and 'we know the size of a volume by
the size of its bounding surfaces.' Van der Laan unfolded his
constructive ordering principles outwards from the individual

dwelling (cell), to the walled courtyard (court), and finally to the collective urban enclosure of town (domain):

> The court is both an outside for the cell and an inside for the domain. This ambivalence of the court enables the inside-outside relation, despite having only two terms, to bind the three separate zones [cell, court, domain] into a whole and bring about the unity of the great inside that is the aim of architecture.

He argued that within the collective town, shaped by bounding walls, 'the marked out domain is not perceived as *form*, but only experienced as an *inside*.'[10] The influence of Van der Laan's concept of wall-bounded 'experience-space' on architects, including Rietveld, Van Eyck, Wiel Arets and Steven Holl, has been profound. Almost twenty years before the publication of his book, Van der Laan's concept was presaged by the Italian architect Carlo Scarpa, who also emphasized the way walls define the space within: 'the sense of space is not communicated by a pictorial order [seen in perspective] but always by a physical phenomena, that is, by matter . . . the weight of the wall.'[11]

The philosopher Martin Heidegger also endeavoured to take the idea of architecture and inhabited interior space back to its origins in a number of his writings, most notably in his 1954 essay 'Building Dwelling Thinking'. He defined human beings as those who dwell, and 'we attain to dwelling, so it seems, only by means of building.' He noted that the old German meaning of building, *Bauen*, is 'to dwell, to stay in a place', and that the ancient Latin meanings of the word to build, *aedificare*, are 'to cultivate' and 'to edify'. He argued that a building does not first come to a place to stand on it, but rather that the place comes into being only by virtue of the building being made there: 'Only things that are places in this manner allow for spaces.' Heidegger drew the key distinction between 'space-in-extension' (parallel to Bergson's 'external and extensive'), which does not allow for human dwelling, and 'place' (parallel to Bergson's 'internal and intensive'), which allows for the space of inhabitation. Heidegger argued that only places allow us to experience space through dwelling: 'Accordingly, spaces [of inhabitation] receive their essential being from places and not from 'space' [in extension].' Buildings are places that found, shape and join together spaces for dwelling within them. To define the space where dwelling takes place, Heidegger used the German word *Raum* (which we have already encountered in Loos's *Raumplan*):

> What the word for space, *Raum*, designates is said by its ancient meaning. *Raum* means a place cleared or freed for settlement and lodging. A space is something that has been made room for, something that is cleared and free, namely, within a boundary, Greek *peras*. A boundary is not that at which something stops but, as the Greeks recognized, the boundary is that from which something *begins its essential unfolding*.[12]

This concept of the interior spatial boundary as an 'essential unfolding', and the dichotomous combination of dimensional imprecision and experiential precision it implies, characterize the constructive ambiguity of layered and overlapping boundaries to be found in many works of Modern architecture, beginning with those of Wright. In the definition of interior rooms, Wright employed multiple boundaries and ambiguous spatial layers, resulting from the overlapping and interpenetration of several spaces. The continuity of the folded planar surfaces of floors and ceilings, and the freestanding walls between them, formed interior space that simultaneously extends and returns upon itself: extending by the projection of space from the hearth at the centre of the house, and returning by the folding of space in the re-entrant corners produced by the folding of walls, ceilings, floors and stairs. Space, defined by multiple layers and overlapping boundaries, is experienced as both deep and shallow, extending into the distance and yet closely bounded. In shaping interior space, Wright argued that the outer edges, walls and terminals forming the boundaries of the space were more important to experience than the definition of the centre: 'Take care of the terminals and the center will take care of itself.'[13]

After visiting Wright's Imperial Hotel, Tokyo, of 1922, Van Eyck in 1966 noted both the way wall masses tended to make even small spaces feel much larger in experience, and the way the folding of Wright's ambiguously bounded spaces produced what he called 'an inner horizon' in experience:

> It is not so much the space that matters as the interior quality of space . . . As you walk up from one floor to another, you carry the horizon of space with you. The horizon is a relative thing, it relates to you, to where you are . . . What matters is not so much space, but the interior of space – and the inner horizon of that interior.

Two years later, when the Imperial Hotel was threatened with destruction, Van Eyck argued for it to be saved by noting:

> The Imperial Hotel has what unfortunately very few contemporary buildings in and outside Japan have: an interior horizon . . . One is subsequently 'received' from space to space and from level to level. This 'interior horizon' can be sensed everywhere . . . Architecture can do no more than assist that reassuring feeling of being interiorized.[14]

Those who inhabit interior space that is enclosed in folding walls interlocked in re-entrant corners experience the space as being simultaneously boundless and bounded. This finds an intriguing parallel in the definition of boundless space given by Wright and Dewey's contemporary the physicist A. S. Eddington: 'Space is boundless by re-entrant form, not by great extension.'[15] In his own winter home and studio, Taliesin West, Wright counterpointed and complemented the ambiguity of the layered and unfolding outer edges of the house by placing large clay pots at strategic spatial joints between interior rooms and exterior courts, where the shadowed volumes formed by their inner walls serve to remind the inhabitants of the essential nature of the vessel enclosing them in the space within.

Like Wright, Le Corbusier also never lost his early focus on the conception of the dwelling as a hollow vessel in which we live – the interior space as a bottle-like container of inhabitation. In describing the design for his own Petit Cabanon (1952), a very small single-room cabin he built on the ocean late in his life, Le Corbusier said: 'the exterior and roof framing are not related to the current problem,' which, as Roberto Gargiani and Anna Rosellini have noted;

> suggests a certain indifference regarding the exterior with respect to his focus on the complex functioning of the residential cell, so much so that the envelope is transformed into [what Le Corbusier called] a sort of 'bag of its skin.'[16]

Similarly, in describing the way he conceived of the interior space actively shaping and forming the interior wall surfaces of the Notre Dame du Haut chapel in Ronchamp (1950–55), Le Corbusier wrote: 'the inside is also an "embossing" but hollow.'[17]

In Le Corbusier's 1948 book *The Modulor*, outlining his system of proportions based on the Golden Section (Fibonacci sequence) and using the human body as the basis for the dimensional divisions, he drew four diagrams of how the Modulor was to be employed: 1) the regulating lines of a facade (simple exterior); 2) a composition combining both urbanism and architecture (complex exterior); 3) his spiralling 'endless museum' design (complex interior); and 4) one of the interior apartments in the Unité d'habitation (simple interior). Gargiani and Rosellini described this fourth diagram of an interior room as

> a cube that is no longer solid, but transparent, woven by a pattern of lines like a modular Japanese interior, at times similar to a

composition of Mondrian or Van Doesburg, or to a work of Concrete Art, or to the 'space modulator' described by Moholy-Nagy.[18]

In characterizing this small interior space (closely related to his Petit Cabanon), Le Corbusier noted that the use of the Modulor to organize the floor, ceiling and wall surfaces would

> create a unitary state of aggregation that may be described as 'textural'. [This would result in an effect] somewhere near the works of nature, which proceed from the inside outwards, uniting, in three dimensions, all the diversity, all the different intentions in perfect harmony.[19]

In their search for the essence of architecture in the experience of the space within, the Irish architects Yvonne Farrell and Shelley McNamara, founding principals of Grafton Architects, have described the place-making power of the thick, protective, space-containing bounding wall, the logic of the social plan and, most important of all, the emotional section – which makes place between earth and sky. Farrell began a 2009 interview by noting:

> In one of his seemingly absurd quotes, [the Spanish architect] Alejandro de la Sota says about architecture: 'One has to achieve as much of nothing as possible.' We understand this 'nothing' as the space in between. The space . . . between the interior and the exterior, between the ground and the sky, as the space containing light, air, and volume, the space where we stand.
>
> The building material is the opposite of 'nothing'. We're interested in something which is 'nothing'. We're interested in the space, the volume, the place. We're interested in transparency, which is in fact layer upon layer of 'nothing' . . . That which is 'nothing' is something.[20]

The hallways outside the classrooms are drawn together and intertwined at the expansive staircase, which projects from the outer wall of the building and into the central courtyard, inviting unplanned meetings and chance encounters. Louis Kahn, Indian Institute of Management, Ahmedabad, India, interior view of staircase landing in classroom hallway; sketch made on 29 March 1984.

Six

The Society of Spaces and the Emplacement of Encounters

Following Wright's initiatory re-establishment of 'the space within' as the fundamental generative concept for Modern architecture, and the subsequent development of the three floor plan types of Wright, Loos and Le Corbusier as different ways of organizing the space of the interior, it may be argued that it was the second-generation Modern architect Louis Kahn who most effectively and influentially engaged the first generation's shared insight that, as he stated it, 'the room is the beginning of architecture,' which Kahn evolved into his design concept, 'the floor plan as a society of spaces'. Kahn's redefinition involved his recognition of the necessity of first establishing the individual character of each room, after which it was possible to re-conceive the composition of the floor plan as the ordering of these independent spaces into a social structure, their spatial relationship articulating the collective institutional purpose of the building:

> I think the most inspirational point from which we might try to understand architecture is to regard the room, the simple room, as the beginning of architecture . . . I think that a plan is a society of spaces. A real plan is one in which rooms have talked to each other . . . The form of a school could have something to do with the conversation of the various rooms, their nature, and how they complement each other and enrich the environment with the feeling of a 'good place to learn'.[1]

In order to be an appropriate place for a given activity, Kahn believed each room should have its own light, its own structure – which he called 'the beginning of containment'[2] – and its own clearly articulated and perceivable spatial boundaries, resulting in each room having a sense of individuality, independence and identity as an element or 'entity' in the society of spaces: 'You might say that the nature of a room is that it always has the character of completeness.'[3] The self-defined, self-centred and self-supporting room-entities were arranged and assembled as independent volumes with individual characters in the larger plan as a society of spaces. For this reason Kahn also believed that people could not truly inhabit what he called the 'division-less space' of the open column grid, and that the plan as a society of spaces required that each room have its own individual qualities of space, structure and light:

> You have a society of rooms in which each one has its character, allowing delicate differences to express themselves. In a way, people meeting in them are different people from those who live in division-less space.[4]

Kahn fundamentally redefined architecture as being ordered not by predetermined floor-area programmes of uses or 'functions' but rather by the poetic interpretation of human actions that take place in the rooms – the making of an individual and independent room-as-place to house each activity: 'The society of rooms is the place where it is good to learn, good to work, good to live.'[5] Rejecting the definition of modern architecture as 'form follows function', and its prescription of strict correspondence between programme functions and the shapes of spaces and plans, Kahn argued against what he considered this literally thoughtless, formulaic beginning for architectural design, stating instead: 'Architecture is the thoughtful making of spaces.'[6] He believed that in the end the most important function of any building was not to be 'functional', at least as it was typically defined, but to 'function psychologically'.[7] Kahn argued that the programming of architectural design should re-engage the full range of human experience and social association so that the resulting buildings enrich, enhance and ennoble the daily life that takes place within their spaces. Kahn called for

> spaces which have as much of a sense of nobility as you can give them. If you look at the Baths of Caracalla . . . we know that we can bathe just as well under an 8-foot ceiling as we can under a 150-foot ceiling, but I believe there's something about a 150-foot ceiling that makes a man a different kind of man.[8]

Kahn's belief that the generosity of interior space directly determined the quality of life that takes place within it is reflected in his telling his students that the level of a 'civilization is measured by the shape and height of your ceiling'.[9]

When Jonas Salk gave Kahn the commission for the Salk Institute for Biological Studies in 1959, he provided only a general and informal outline of the spatial requirements, and instead asked Kahn to design a place where he could invite the painter Pablo Picasso to meet his scientists. Based on this experience, Kahn argued: 'I believe it is the duty of every architect . . . not to accept programs but to think in terms of spaces,' and stated that architecture 'is not the filling of areas prescribed by the client. It is the creating of spaces that evoke a feeling of appropriate use.'[10] This involved the architect changing the prescribed areas of the programme into spaces that are 'good for the institution . . . He must change corridors into galleries; he must change lobbies into places of entrance.'[11] Kahn noted that in buildings that followed the formula of predetermined typologies and prescribed functional programmes, the rooms were both uninspired in their design and uninspiring to those who occupied them. Instead, he argued that rooms should be designed with a poetic understanding of human actions as inspired: 'I make a space as an offering, and do not designate what it is to be used for. The use should be inspired.' He then noted that designing went beyond simply meeting the programme requirements, as for an entrance foyer in a dormitory:

> I have not simply made an entrance, but a meeting place . . . What I did was to make the entrance room equally as important as a dining room, a living room; that central entity in the ground plan became the entrance meeting place.[12]

Kahn believed that the most important room in a building was often not named in the programme of spaces given to the architect, and that it was the responsibility of the architect to argue for this space, which he called the 'room with no name'.[13] In Kahn's Salk Institute, the central courtyard between the laboratory buildings is a travertine-paved 'façade to the sky', as the landscape architect Luis Barragán called it,[14] with a linear watercourse aligning with the sunset, the walls framing a view of the ocean and horizon at its end – none of which was part of the formal programme of spaces. Yet the building is unimaginable without the courtyard, its most important room and one of the most powerful and deeply moving spaces ever built. In a similar way, the top-lit central entry hall of Kahn's Exeter Library (1965–72), rising the full height of the building and framed by large circular openings revealing the book stacks on all four sides, celebrating the purpose of the building, was absent from the programme of spaces Kahn was given at the start of the project – a room with no name without which the Library, as it stands today, is simply inconceivable. In this room, Kahn realized his ideal, articulated in thinking about the work of Le Corbusier: 'A glorious central and single space, the walls and their light left in faceted planes, the shapes of the record of their making, intermingled with the serenity of light from above.'[15]

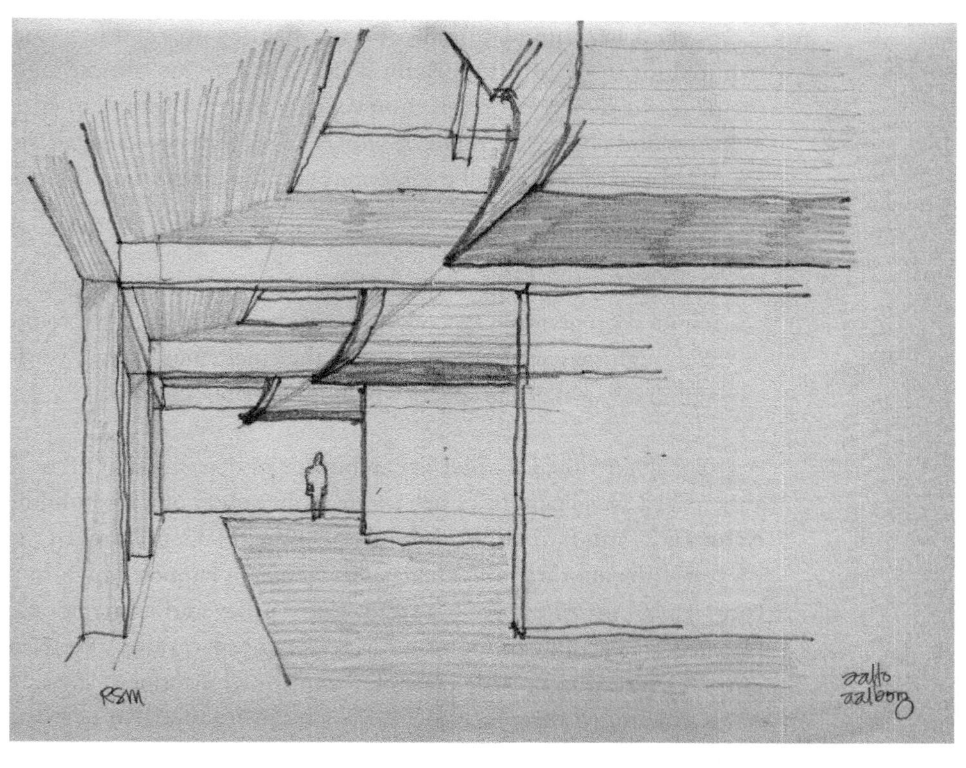

Parallel galleries arranged to invite wandering movement paths bathed in natural light, with multiple intersections and thresholds joining a society of spaces. Alvar Aalto, Kunsten Museum of Modern Art Aalborg, Denmark, interior of galleries with skylights and suspended shells; sketch made on 27 September 1983.

Beyond accommodating the specific planned uses and functions required for the institution, Kahn believed the rooms composing the plan as a society of spaces should make places for unplanned meetings and chance encounters, which Kahn considered essential for the inspiration of social interactions and meetings of individuals in the space within:

> You can have ordered relationships of other conveniences [the required programme spaces], but those are all in the background, as though they were the servants of the emergence of little worlds within a world of the spaces which interrelate.[16]

Arguing against the idea that the architect can determine or even anticipate a social pattern of behaviour in the spaces of their building, Kahn said: 'You have no idea about the individual, and in what way, meeting another individual, something can happen which is completely unpredictable.'[17] Instead, Kahn believed that the floor plan was an assembly of rooms into a society of spaces that interrelate in such a way as to provide places for unplanned meetings.

Kahn argued that the individual room-entity is related to the society of spaces by 'the places of entrance, the galleries that radiate from them, the intimate entrances to the spaces of the institution [which] form an independent architecture of connection'.[18] This connecting architecture consisted of the spaces of movement – thresholds, foyers, vestibules, hallways, arcades, intersections, porches, staircases and their landings – which Kahn called the experiential 'events of the building',[19] and which he believed were generative of unstructured socializing and unplanned meetings. He held that the architecture of connection was as important to the overall experience of the building as the primary spaces given in the programme: 'The institution is truly an inspired place by reason of the entrance, the galleries of movement, and the harbors leading to the various spaces. This is the measure of the architect.'[20]

A particularly telling example of Kahn's concept of the plan as a society of spaces are the classrooms of his Indian Institute of Management in Ahmedabad, India (1962–74), which are connected by entrance foyers that overlap with the wide arcaded hallway along the edge of the building's central court, so that the foyers are equal in size to the classrooms they serve, and are better illuminated and ventilated. This resulted from Kahn's belief that in designing

> a school as a realm of spaces where it is good to learn, the lobby measured by the institute as so many square feet per student would become a generous Pantheon-like space where it is good to enter. The corridors would be transformed into classrooms belonging to the students themselves . . . [a place] where the student discusses the work of the professor with a fellow student . . . which means a place of possibilities in self-learning.[21]

In her book *Frank Lloyd Wright's Living Space* the sociologist Gail Satler argues that the invariably isolated viewpoints of sociology and architectural history have failed to recognize the fundamentally social structure of Wright's interior spaces. Wright understood that 'architecture was a living expression – "the space within to be lived in"', and Satler maintains this could only be realized 'from a vantage point that was rooted in the reality of everyday life. That meant seeing and working from within rather than taking a stance that was external to and removed from the collective experience.' She holds that inherent in Wright's architecture 'is the notion that space is more than physical. It is intensely and essentially social.' She defines her concept of 'Wright's living space' by noting: 'What gives space life [is] the aspect of a building that only exists by people using and experiencing it.' Satler argues that Wright's work is experienced as a place where inhabitants are allowed to take their own stance and determine their own direction: 'The interior "space within to be lived in" moves us to a place where greater inclusion, interaction, and sociability are possible.' She notes:

> Architecture, for all practical purposes, is defined as it relates to the needs and desires of people and by their changing positions within that space. This is the freedom and at the same time the sense of shelter that Wright really sought to achieve and to convey to inhabitants of his buildings.[22]

Wright's pivotal social concept in design, according to Satler, was his transformation of spatial 'enclosure' into experiential 'shelter', which she argued is intimately connected to Wright's emphasis on the essential horizontality of interior spaces:

> What was being created was a place that housed the unlimited potential for fulfilling needs – ones in which the limits are set by inhabitants . . . In horizontal structures, solutions emerge from the interaction and coexistence of differences. A solution is derived through interaction . . . rather than through imposition of one view.[23]

Satler juxtaposed the unlimited potential and social interaction in horizontal structures to the imposition of limits and social hierarchy generally associated with vertical structures. Wright's Larkin Building of 1904, while a vertical office building of multiple floors, nevertheless is constructed of horizontal, expansive spaces of the type Satler described: spaces which provided a sense of shelter and freedom of movement for the inhabitants. The collective experience within the building was centred on the vertical atrium, which, rather than imposing a hierarchical spatial or social structure was deployed to allow the office workers, who were accommodated on the spacious middle floors, to overlook the company executives, who occupied the ground floor. The top floor, normally the province of the executives in an office building, was instead occupied by the employee restaurant, where Wright emphasized the collective attitude of the company by designing the dining tables with raised posts at their narrow ends, so that it was not possible for anyone, including the executives, who took their meals with the employees, to sit at the 'head' of the table.

The precision with which Wright orchestrated the movements and interactions of people within his spaces – the experiential encounters engendered and invited by the structure of the space within – serves to exemplify what might best be called erotic space, as it was defined by the architectural critic and historian Robin Evans in his classic essay of 1978, 'Figures, Doors and Passages'. Evans begins his essay with a section entitled 'The Plan and its Occupants', noting:

> If anything is described by an architectural plan, it is the nature of human relationships, since the elements whose trace it records – walls, doors, windows and stairs – are employed first to divide and then selectively to re-unite inhabited space.[24]

Evans re-reads the history of architecture since the Renaissance as the evolution of ways in which the plan can encourage and invite, or discourage and delimit, encounters among the inhabitants – how exactly human figures occupy the spaces within.

Evans notes that, prior to the last two hundred years, connected rooms in buildings were invariably joined by multiple doorways, either in a labyrinthine interlacing like a quilt, or in a line, called an *enfilade*, whereby rooms are strung like beads along a thread. These plans, where one must move through rooms to reach other rooms, all indicate 'the fondness for company, proximity and incident' on the part of their inhabitants – 'incident' being the encounters with other inhabitants that Kahn had called 'unplanned meetings'. Evans noted how these plans 'made visible a corporeal attraction that drew people together for no reason outside of desire'. In counterpoint to these interconnected rooms were the floor plans, first appearing two hundred years ago, which employed a corridor onto which each room opened through a single door:

> No longer was it necessary to pass through the intractable occupied territory of rooms, with all the diversions, incidents and accidents that they might harbor. Instead, the door of any room would deliver you into a network of routes from which the room next door and the furthest extremity of the house were equally accessible. In other words, these corridors were able to draw distant rooms closer, but only by disengaging those near at hand . . . in facilitating communication, the corridor reduced contact.

This tendency reached its high point, according to Evans, in Alexander Klein's prototype house of 1928, called 'The Functional House for Frictionless Living', where Evans notes that the inhabitants' 'paths literally never cross'. The name Klein gave his early modern domestic prototype 'implied that all accidental encounters caused friction and therefore threatened the smooth running of the domestic machine'.[25]

Evans concludes by tracing the more recent development of floor plans organized with corridors and one-door rooms, which emphasize functional separation and individual privacy: 'the corridor plan, which is appropriate to a society that finds carnality distasteful, which sees the body as a vessel of mind and spirit, and in which privacy is habitual'. He contrasts this type of plan, which he notes 'limits the horizon of experience', to floor plans, both ancient and modern, which are characterized by what may be called the familial relations of connected rooms that open to each other, and that engender and invite chance encounters and embodied experiences:

> The matrix of connected rooms is appropriate to a type of society that feeds on carnality, which recognizes the body as the person, and in which gregariousness is habitual.

Though Evans finds that the general tendency over the last two hundred years has been the increased predominance of the corridor plan, the opposite type of floor plan – the kind that makes places for encounters – typifies the *plan libre* of Le Corbusier, the *Raumplan* of Loos and the 'woven plan' of Wright. In the Dana House of 1900, Wright made no corridors, gave all the rooms – including the master bedroom – more than one door, and opened all the rooms to each other, so that one must move through rooms to reach other rooms. Evans describes this kind of plan as belonging to

> an architecture arising out of the deep fascination that draws people towards others; an architecture that recognizes passion, carnality and sociality. The matrix of interconnected rooms might well be an integral feature of such buildings.[26]

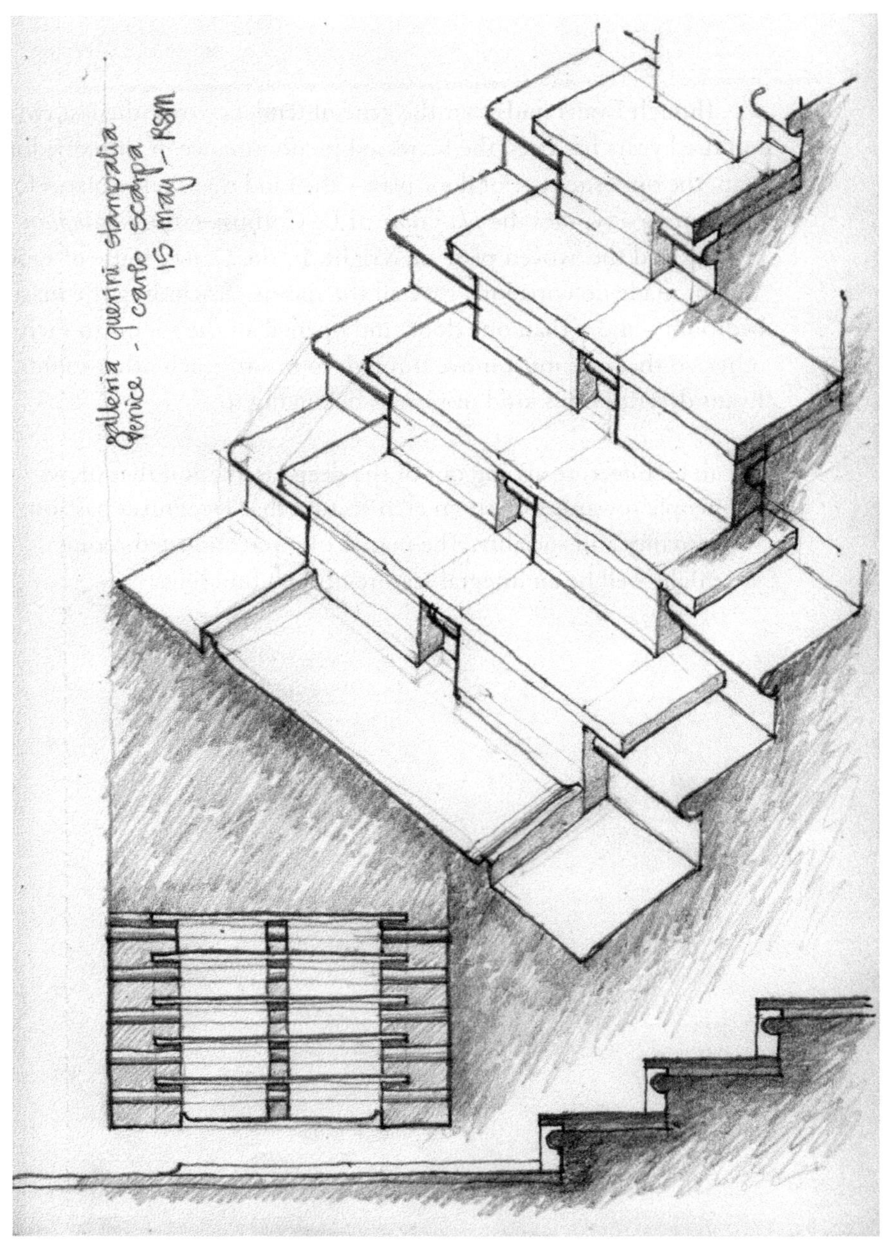

New stair treads inscribed into an old staircase, allowing the inhabitants to experience the dense layering of time and the intimate nesting of space. Carlo Scarpa, Fondazione Querini Stampalia, Venice, Italy, interior stairs up to library; sketch made on 15 May 1984.

Seven

The Nesting of Places at Once Intimate and Immense

The interior experience of the room that is composed of a nesting of spaces is at once intimate and immense, connecting us to the cosmos at the same moment as it grounds us in the tactile touch. Antonello da Messina's painting *St Jerome in his Study* presents a view of the saint sitting at a wooden desk, set within a raised wooden room, with his books and intimate belongings surrounding him and within easy reach. This double-layered wooden-walled room, small and intimate, warm to the touch and sheltering the body, in turn stands within a larger, taller, massive masonry-walled space that is cold, hard and uninviting to touch, which is itself one bay of a multi-bayed sanctuary structure. The way in which the entire space, from the individual body scale of the built-in furnishings to the collective public scale of the stone vaulting of the monastery church, are all precisely scaled by and ordered by the interior experience of the inhabitant – the saint at work in his study – makes this a definitive demonstration of the conception of simultaneous intimacy and immensity in the space within.

The examination of the experience of inhabiting the space within, the related concepts of intimacy and immensity in interior rooms, and the literal embodiment of human experience in archi-tecture which has proven to be the most inspiring for architects and critics during the last fifty years is to be found in the French philosopher Gaston Bachelard's book *The Poetics of Space.*[1] Bachelard prefaced his investigation by arguing for the primacy of the human body and its position in the experience of interior space: 'To curl up belongs to the phenomenology of the verb to inhabit, and only those who have learned to do so can inhabit with intensity.' Bachelard begins with the house as the single best source for the 'study of the intimate values of inside space', and he holds that contemporary philosophers of dwelling (clearly meaning Heidegger, though Bachelard does not name him) were mistaken: 'Before he is "cast into the world," as claimed by certain hasty metaphysics, man is laid in the cradle of the house.' He also holds (in contra-distinction to Benjamin's interpretation of experience as 'distraction') that the repeated experience of the interior space of the house, rather than becoming routinely habitual, 'has engraved within us the hierarchy of the various functions of inhabiting . . . The word habit is too worn a word to express this passionate liaison of our bodies, which do not forget, with an unforgettable house.'[2]

Bachelard examines the poetic experiences of the house, establishing its two primary themes of verticality, 'ensured by the polarity of the cellar and attic' and exemplifying 'the dramatic tension between the aerial and the terrestrial', and centrality, as 'a concentrated being' and 'a world in itself'.[3] Bachelard moves from the cellar to the attic in his exploration of the part the archetypal interior rooms and spaces of the house play in both our dreams and our waking ruminations. For Bachelard, 'the significance of the hut' is that the memories of our childhood home and its interior spaces are carried with us throughout our life, the experiences gained within those spaces forming the basis for assessing all other spaces we later inhabit. Our memories of the interior spaces of our house are transformed as the result of our ever-changing mood, as is revealed in Georges Spyridaki's description of the syncopated experience of intimacy and immensity within his house:

> My house is diaphanous, but it is not of glass . . . Its walls contract and expand as I desire. At times, I draw them close about me like protective armor . . . But at others, I let the walls of my house blossom out in their own space, which is infinitely extensible.[4]

In the simultaneity of intimacy and immensity of interior space, Bachelard notes that the house also may be said both to contain and to be the universe, and he explores poetic responses to the inhabitable spaces of furniture, drawers, chests and wardrobes. Bachelard notes: 'A house that has been experienced is not an inert box. Inhabited space transcends geometrical space.' When inhabiting an interior space, 'quite paradoxically, even cubic dimensions have no more meaning, for the reason that a new dimension – the dimension of intimacy – has just opened up'. And, from the perspective of the inhabitant, 'this dimension can be an infinite one.' Bachelard's definition of intimacy as a fundamentally interior condition is indicated by his dichotomous pairing of 'exterior and intimacy', as well as his caution that those who wish to study the experience of inhabitation 'must not be subject to the charms of external beauty. For generally, beauty exteriorizes and disturbs intimate meditation.'[5]

Bachelard recalls the way in which Victor Hugo had written in *Notre-Dame de Paris* that, for Quasimodo, the cathedral was

> successively egg, nest, house, country, universe . . . One might almost say that he had taken on its shape, as a snail does that of its shell. It was his dwelling-place, his stronghold, his envelope . . . He adhered to it, as it were, like a turtle to its carapace. The rugged cathedral was his armor . . . the strange, symmetrical, immediate, almost consubstantial flexibility of a man and an edifice.[6]

Bachelard's exploration of the parallels between the interior spaces of human houses and those found in animal nests and shells centres on bodily presence as it is involved in the shaping of enclosures. In describing the relationship between the human body and the 'nest' embodied by the space within, Bachelard notes that, in Jules Michelet's study of birds, *L'Oiseau* of 1858, the author

> suggests a house built by and for the body, taking form from the inside, like a shell, is an intimacy that works physically. The form of the nest is commanded by the inside . . . Everything is a matter of inner pressure, physically dominant intimacy . . . pressing against its limits.

In this 'purely physical intimacy' of the body enclosed within its nest-like interior room, the experience 'expresses the function of inhabiting in terms of touch'.[7]

In his exploration of inner corners and the capacity of small, body-sized interior spaces to engender inhabitation, Bachelard points out: 'every corner in a house, every angle in a room, every inch of secluded space in which we like to . . . withdraw into ourselves . . . is the germ of a room.' He goes on to note how 'the beloved corner has nest-like powers; it incites us to possession, it is . . . inhabited geometry.' The nesting of space-within-space, and the resulting miniature world-within-a-world that is created for the inhabitants, is exemplified for Bachelard by the light cast upon the table in the darkness of night: 'The evening lamp on the family table is also the center of a world. In fact, the lamp-lighted table is a little world in itself.' This deeply shadowed domestic world relies less on sight than on the smells of the meal, the sounds of voices and the touch of hands on the wooden table, and Bachelard argues: 'Sight curtails the dramas it witnesses,' but a smell or sound 'can create an entire environment'.[8] This observation is paralleled by that of the architect Herman Hertzberger, who points out that in Vincent van Gogh's *The Potato Eaters* of 1885,

A lamp hanging over the table accurately defines the centre of
attention [of those gathered around the table]. The light it sheds
. . . enables people and their attributes to jointly shape the space,
so that there is ultimately a fusion between people and place
. . . [so that] people and place complement each other.[9]

Bachelard's study of interior, inhabited space hinges on two
concluding conceptual pairings, the first being that of intimacy
and immensity. In the chapter titled 'intimate immensity', he argues
that both intimate and immense scales of experience characterize
memorable rooms. He notes how, like the forest, an interior room
'accumulates its infinity within its own boundaries' and that a
place 'invested with intimate space becomes the center of all space'
for its occupants, and that in their experience 'the horizon exists
as much as the center'.[10] In this Bachelard parallels the American
Transcendentalist writer Ralph Waldo Emerson, who noted in
regards to inhabitation and experience: 'People forget that the eye
makes the horizon.'[11] Bachelard points out that, in his descriptions
of the immensity of interior space in experience, the poet Baudelaire
used the word 'vast' more than any other word: 'vast is one of the
most Baudelairian of words, the word that marks most naturally,
for this poet, infinity of intimate space.' This observation is complemented by Bachelard's own favoured word in this study, 'intimate',
as indicated by his definition: 'immensity in the intimate domain is
intensity, an intensity of being, the intensity of being evolving in
the vast perspective of intimate immensity.'[12]

Bachelard's second concluding pairing of concepts is that of
outside and inside (which will be examined in the final chapter
of this book). He begins by noting that, while 'from the point
of view of geometrical expressions, the dialectics of outside and
inside is supported by a reinforced geometrism, in which limits
are barriers,' interior experience mitigates against understanding
outside and inside as opposites. This is exemplified by the experience

of entering or leaving a room, for 'to go in and come out are never symmetrical images,' and the doorway or threshold has always been experienced as a sacred place. While inhabited interior and exterior spaces are not experienced as being separated by strict geometrical barriers, the sensitive surface of the room between inside and outside is critical to our ability to perceive both spaces. When the surface is broken or erased in our experience of interior space, 'intimate space loses its clarity, while exterior space loses its void, void being the raw material of possibility of being.' Bachelard notes that in the conception of a room, 'the two terms "outside" and "inside" . . . are not symmetrical. To make inside concrete and outside vast is the first task . . . Outside and inside are both intimate.' Bachelard concludes by arguing that, in experience, the space within and the inhabitant become one, and, paralleling Wright, holds that to allow the inhabitants to experience repose is the most important function of the room:

> The intimacy of the room becomes our intimacy . . . The room is very deeply our room, it is in us. We no longer *see* it. It no longer *limits* us, because we are in the very ultimate depth of its repose, in the repose that it has conferred on us.[13]

Attentiveness to both intimacy and immensity may be said to characterize the modern architects whose works remain in our memory owing to their acute sensitivity to the subtleties of experience. This results from architects being deeply involved in the design of interior spaces that possess the quality of both immensity, connecting us to earth and sky and distant horizon, and intimacy, surrounding us with appropriately scaled surfaces and details that we engage at first hand, and which impart to immense spaces an intimate, embodied scale. As Bachelard notes: 'Everything, even size, is a human value,' and both immensity and intimacy are scaled to the human being in its embodied experience.[14]

The anthropologist Edward T. Hall, whose writings were instrumental in bringing recognition to the importance of fundamental patterns of human perception in the experience of architectural spaces, notes: 'Much of Frank Lloyd Wright's success as an architect was due to his recognition of the many different ways in which people experience space.'[15] This is paralleled, with particular relevance for the pairing of immensity and intimacy, by more recent studies of the critical relationship between neuroscience and architecture, including those of the architectural historian Harry Mallgrave. Wright's Prairie houses, with their densely interwoven and ambiguously bounded spaces, were presented by Mallgrave as excellent architectural examples of 'ambiguity' as it has been defined in the writings of the neurobiologist Semir Zeki. According to Zeki, in cognition, the human brain tends to spend little time or cognitive energy on easily categorized or familiar events, and instead is engaged and challenged by events or elements that have multiple, equally valid meanings or interpretations, and which as a result activate a number of different areas of the brain, including not only perception, but learning, judgement, memory and experience.[16]

The ambiguity typical of Wright's Prairie period designs was the result of his constructing multiple boundary definitions and multiple spatial interpretations. Paradoxically, this experiential ambiguity was the result of the strict geometric order in plan, both in the underlying grid and in the shapes of the rooms, which was Wright's primary method of structuring his 'woven plans'. This spatial structure enabled Wright's spaces to be both independent, as pure geometric volumes, and interdependent, as part of a continuous spatial fusion. He assembled proportionally related volumes into spatial clusters, and the relationship of the underlying square grid to the occupied spaces was of utmost importance. Wright considered the modular volumes of each space capable of being articulated and structured individually and independently – as he wrote, the different rooms 'may thus become small buildings in themselves',[17] each with its own structure and symmetrical order. Wright's Prairie period buildings were frequently composed of several symmetrical, self-defined independent rooms that were interlocked along their major and minor axes to form larger symmetrical or asymmetrical wholes.

Wright employed the concept of 'nesting' spaces – smaller spaces set within larger rooms – so that his buildings were composed of similar elements repeated at varying scales. The nested forms and spaces were invariably designed using the same ordering principles, resulting in a hierarchy of carefully scaled elements shaping the space of inhabitation. His furniture, both freestanding and built-in, was often developed as an 'interpretation' or 'variation on the theme' of the building as a whole; as an example, the wooden sideboard in the Robie House dining room is a reduced-scale version of the main street facade of the house. The major structural piers of Wright's Prairie houses were invariably paired, and the space between them was defined by a smaller, inset pair of piers, together shaping a series of nested habitable volumes from the scale of the building down to the scale of the individual. Complementing this nesting of similarly proportioned spaces was Wright's interweaving of spaces of differing proportions, as in the Evans House (1908), where a series of piers of different heights are projected different lengths from the cubic central volume to form a series of nested horizontal planes and multiple bounding edges.

The experience of simultaneous intimacy and immensity of interior spaces in Wright's buildings was the result of the interweaving of space-defining planes of floors, walls and ceilings; the nesting of spaces inside spaces at varying scales; and the resulting sense of spatial contraction and exfoliation – what Dewey called 'retracting' and 'unfolding'.[18] Employing these common methods, Wright evolved complementary and contrasting spatial experiences for public and private buildings. The interior experience of Wright's

Unity Temple is at once immense, where one is enclosed by the folding and unfolding of cubic geometries around the periphery, where one's attention is focused on the vertical central volume that opened up and out to connect to the sky, and where inhabitants are suspended in an ethereal light from above; and intimate, where all inhabitants are enmeshed by a weaving of thin lines in space, where the nesting of planes form dense layers of enclosure near at hand, and where all inhabitants are drawn close together, allowing each to recognize the others as members of a family gathered for worship. The interior experience of Wright's Darwin Martin House is at once immense, where the interweaving fabric of floors, beams and ceilings shape space that extends outwards in all directions under broad overhanging roof eaves, connecting each occupant to the distant horizon; and intimate, where the thick layering of walls, piers, lead-lined windows and wood cabinetry shapes nested spaces-within-spaces clustered around the massive solid hearth at the centre of the house.

In the achievement of simultaneous intimacy and immensity in the space within, the nesting of spaces and interpreting of individual rooms as small buildings within the larger building is an ancient conception, one that was articulated by the Renaissance architect Leon Battista Alberti:

> If (as the philosophers maintain) the city is like some large house, and the house in turn is like some small city, cannot the various parts [rooms] of the house – atria, xysti, dining rooms, porticos, and so on – be considered miniature buildings?[19]

Among modern architects, it was Louis Kahn who most literally gave embodied form to Alberti's concept. The Fort Wayne Performing Arts Center (1966–73) was conceived by Kahn as a building-within-a-building, with what he called the 'violin' – the acoustically determined auditorium, enclosed by complexly folded, self-supporting cast concrete walls – set within the 'violin case' – the lobby, access stairs and foyer, a separate structure constructed of concrete block and brick that surrounded and protected the auditorium within. Kahn employed a similar nested concept in the design of Exeter Library, where the outer brick-structured building houses the small wood reading room carrels at the periphery, within which is the concrete-structured building that houses the larger horizontal book stack rooms, which in turn are wrapped around so as to form the top-lit vertical entry hall at the building's centre.

Kahn's nesting of buildings-within-buildings, and the concomitant intimate immensity of experience, may be said to reach its climax in the Assembly Building of his Bangladesh National Capital at Dhaka (1962–74). Here Kahn constructed a clustered series of room-buildings that were each given a remarkable level of independence, allowing him to characterize his arrangement as similar to placing individual chess pieces on a chessboard. The Assembly Building is an intensely nested spatial composition constructed of no fewer than eight layers of walls, forming eight types of spaces, extending from the outer wall of the surrounding lake to the inner wall of the central assembly hall itself. Eight independent room-buildings – a prayer hall, entry hall, meeting rooms and dining rooms, and four office blocks – are gathered around the central assembly hall, and the outer and inner spaces are separated and joined by the ambulatory atrium space that rises from the ground floor to the roof. As one moves through the building, one discovers that top light is introduced into five of the eight spatial layers: in eight square light courts at the outer offices, in four cylindrical light towers at the outer corners of the prayer hall, along the entire length of the encircling ambulatory atrium, in eight triangular light courts surrounding the assembly hall, and in the central assembly hall itself. As a result, the nesting of rooms-within-rooms within the building surrounds the inhabitant with layers of lighted and shadowed walls, providing both extended

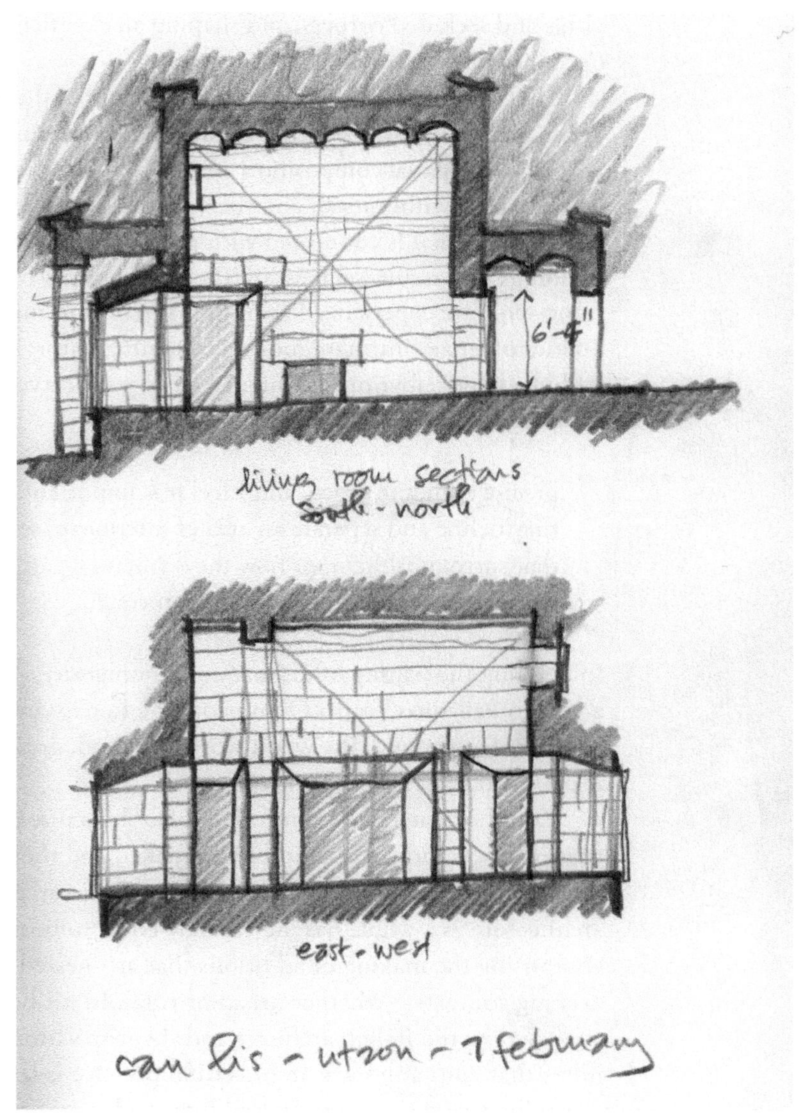

Living room overlooking the sea, set beneath a shell-like roof and walls, with nest-like windows carved through massive thickness and extending out to frame distant views, making the experience at once intimate and immense. Jørn Utzon, Can Lis, Mallorca, Spain, sections of living room, south–north (top) and east–west (bottom); sketch made on 7 February 2015.

vistas and secluded corners, and shaping an experience that is at once intimate and immense.

The Swiss architect Peter Zumthor noted that the most engaging experiences take place within buildings that are composed using two kinds of spatial composition: 'the closed architectural body that isolates space within itself, and the open body that embraces the area of space that is connected with the endless continuum'. The buildings that result, such as his Therme (thermal baths) at Vals (1990–96), are experienced as both intimate and immense, with a series of small, intimate rooms containing baths, which are set within a larger labyrinthine interlacing of walls carved into the earth. Zumthor called the individual rooms

> precise bodies in space, and I feel it is important to sense how they define and separate an area of interior space from the space that surrounds them, or how they contain a part of the infinite spatial continuum in a kind of open vessel.

In defining the pairing of intimacy and immensity, Zumthor recalled a visit to Palladio's Teatro Olimpico: 'The Renaissance theater in Vicenza. Steep rows. The wood worn and aged, great intimacy. A powerful sense of space, intensity.'[20]

Zumthor entered the profession of architecture after first being trained as a woodworker and cabinetmaker, and then practising as a preservation architect. In parallel to Zumthor's career, contemporary architecture as a whole has increasingly come to be understood as comprising the making of additions that are 'nested' within pre-existing contexts – whether urban or rural. In his book *Inside Architecture*, the Italian architect and theorist Vittorio Gregotti notes that contemporary architectural practice is less about designing freestanding object buildings and more about nesting new buildings inside existing buildings:

building within the built . . . Every architectural operation increasingly becomes an act of partial transformation within a situation: reuse, restoration, but also something new and different through the contextual relationship of already significant materials.[21]

This concept of nesting a new space inside an old space was the way the Italian architect Carlo Scarpa defined his practice. Scarpa's designs involved layering new walls into old walls, weaving historical and contemporary fabric to construct rooms that were intimate and immense in both their spatial and experiential characters. Inhabiting Scarpa's renovation of the Fondazione Querini Stampalia (1961–3), we realize that we are never far from the water of Venice, which, in reality and by implication, appears beneath and beside us at every point in our perambulations. This begins in the entry hall, where the shimmering, geometrically patterned marble floor, reminiscent of the floors of ancient Venetian churches, is surrounded by a moat-like trench that contains the *acqua alta* – high water – and thus allows the room, whose floor was well below the flood line, to be used in all seasons. Even when dry, the curb and trench serve as a reminder in all seasons of the intimate relation of the city of Venice to the water. Protected by this moat, the pier-like walkways conduct us to a sunken room whose walls are framed in travertine stone, in which a hinged stone door is opened, which leads onwards to the garden behind the building. The floor of the garden is raised to allow trees to grow in the saltwater-saturated ground, and a watercourse runs from east to west, reminding the inhabitant of the historical flow of influence from the East to Venice. As Michael Cadwell noted: 'Scarpa's was an aquatic sensibility, saturated by Venice.'[22]

Adolf Loos's Kärntner or 'American' Bar in Vienna (1908), though a remarkably small room, combined in experience the visual immensity of the infinite reflections of the coffered marble ceiling in the above-eye-level mirrors, and the physical intimacy of nestling one's body into the low leather banquettes – two experiences usually considered mutually exclusive. The Austrian architect Peter Noever recalled Scarpa's first visit to Loos's room:

> We had hardly entered when [Scarpa] began to express his passionate admiration for what he saw. Gradually his eyes wandered from the ceiling – which had caught his attention first – into the room itself. He noticed the women who were sitting at the bar, approached them, and bowed with a smile. At once he found himself the center of a group of people who quite obviously were interested in everything but architecture. Scarpa ordered champagne for them and a measuring tape for himself. He was fascinated by Adolf Loos and his architecture. He joked with the guests as he surveyed every detail of the room with his eyes and hands. He assumed unexpected positions, and eventually started – with the aid of the ladies – to take exact measurements of the 'Loos' bar. He was inspired by the proportions and details and wanted to know the diameter of the bar rail down to the last millimeter. He finally proclaimed the room a place of 'singular spiritual and emotional quality.'[23]

The work of Alvar Aalto is exemplary of the strong grounding of the interior spaces of Modern architecture in the fusion of intimacy and immensity, orchestrated in his buildings by scaling selected architectural surfaces and elements through the deployment of materials that invite our touch – both physical and visual. In the immense, seemingly infinite field of tiny pieces of pine that make up the ceiling of the living room of the Villa Mairea (1937–9), each with a small elliptical aperture drilled through to allow ventilation to permeate the room; the wood slat and rattan wrapping of the clustered steel columns that, along with the wood poles surrounding the staircase, relate the interior to the vertical trunks of the forest outside the large windows; and the intimate, singular handle on the sauna door, made of a polished forked branch, Aalto may be said to have engaged the intertwining of intimacy and immensity to be found in his friend Georges Braque's concept of 'tactile space'.

Examples of modern interior spaces that are at once intimate and immense, engaging the qualities Bachelard presented in his book, would include the Petit Cabanon of Le Corbusier, which was the architect's place of retreat from the civilized world into the intimacies of primitive interior life – a space precisely proportioned and scaled to house his own body and that of his wife, Yvonne – complemented by the apertures opened above the worktable that give a view of the infinite expanse of the ocean horizon outside. It is interesting to note that, at the same time he was designing and building the intimate space of the Petit Cabanon, Le Corbusier was evolving, in works such as the chapel at Ronchamp and the monastery of La Tourette, his conception of profound and emotionally resonant interior space, which he called 'ineffable space', with its clear intimations of immensity and infinity.

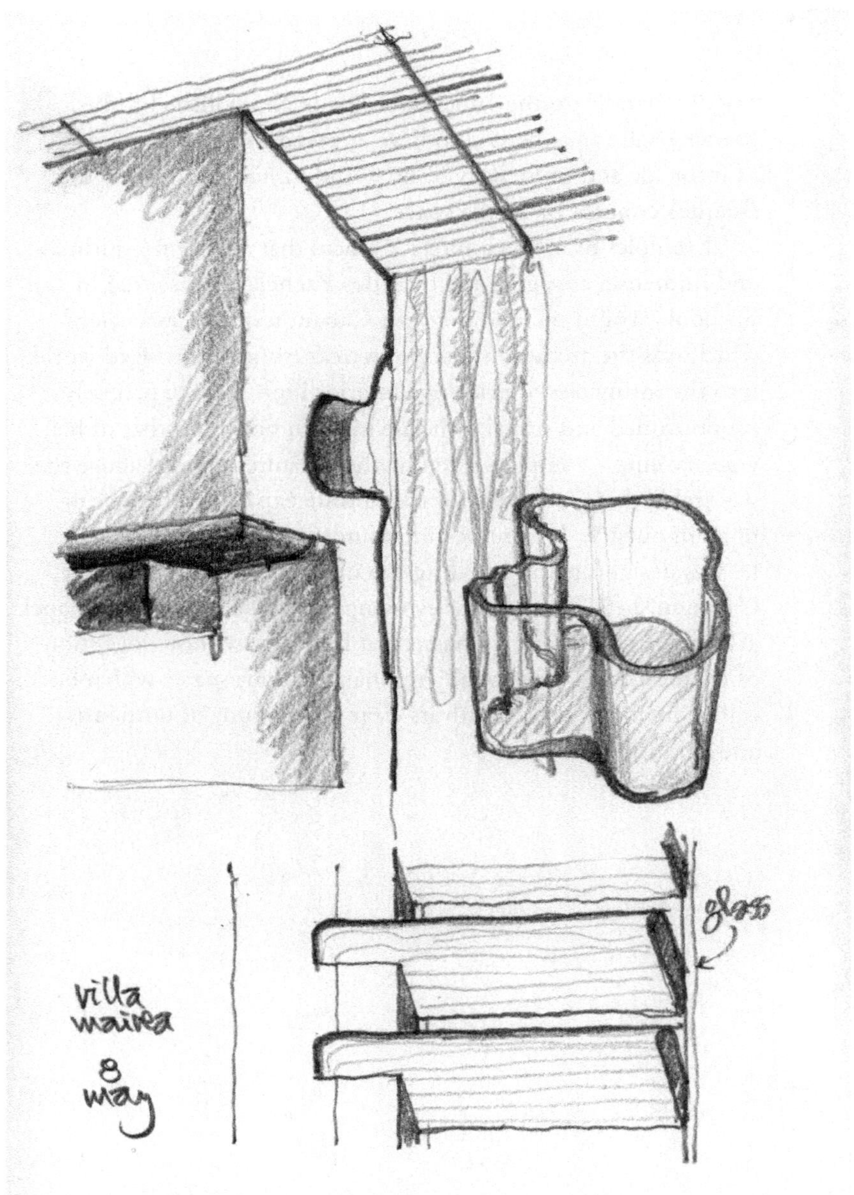

Curving forms carved from the white mass of the fireplace, as if made of snow, matching
curves formed by a glass vase, as if made of ice, combine to subtly recall the Finnish winter
in a summerhouse. Alvar Aalto, Villa Mairea, Noormarkku, Finland, interior details of fireplace,
window, glass vase and garden room door at corner of living room; sketch made on 8 May 2001.

Eight

Making Room for Experience and Memory

The primacy of interior space in Modern architecture involves the recognition that a room that is designed to appropriately enrich experience has profound immediate and long-lasting effects on those who dwell within it, as reflected in their embodied memories of those experiences, and the way those spaces both house and shape their actions. Lived experiences and recollected memories are most movingly and lastingly embodied within rooms conceived as places of inhabitation: rooms that provide their inhabitants with a simultaneous sense of extending out to connect to the distant horizon and withdrawing into close places of repose; rooms anchored to their sites and thereby integrated into the history and nature of their place; rooms resonant with the memory of their making, legible in their structure, materials and joinery; rooms brought to life by the play of light throughout the day, the season and the year; and rooms tailored precisely to the rituals of daily life that take place within them. In describing the power of what he called 'fixed-feature' space – a room engendering both habitual use and embodied memory – on the lives of inhabitants, Edward Hall noted:

> it is the mold into which a great deal of behavior is cast. It was this feature of space that the late Sir Winston Churchill referred to when he said: 'We shape our buildings and they shape us.' During the debate on restoring the House of Commons after

the war, Churchill feared that departure from the intimate spatial pattern of the House, where opponents face each other across a narrow aisle, would seriously alter the patterns of government.[1]

The relation between the space within and the experience and memory of the inhabitant is a deeply moving one, and the atmosphere or mood of a room can have a profound effect on the behaviour and temperament of the inhabitant. Juhani Pallasmaa has observed:

> The impact of a room on our memory can be forceful . . . The space is internalized as an embodied experience and the body scheme and its basic system of orientation (front and behind, above and below, left and right) is projected onto the room and its perimeters. A memorable room becomes part of me, and I leave parts of myself in the room.[2]

Pallasmaa points out that both people's memory and identity are inextricably tied to the interior spaces in which their lives take place: 'We understand and remember who we are primarily through our settings and constructions, both material and mental.' He writes that rooms serve

> as memory devices in three different ways: first, they materialize and preserve the course of time and make it visible; second, they concretize remembrance by containing and projecting memories; third, they stimulate and inspire us to reminisce and imagine.[3]

The poet Noël Arnaud wrote, 'I am the space, where I am', and Pallasmaa notes how this concise and condensed statement makes clear 'the intertwining of world and self as well as the externalized ground of remembrance and identity'.[4]

In his 1896 study of the relation between present perception and the recollection of the past, *Matter and Memory*, Henri Bergson maintained: 'there is no perception which is not full of memories.' Similarly to Hall, Bergson held that memory is fundamentally a habit embedded in the living body, and that in this 'habit memory' the body's past is enacted in the present: 'it is part of my present, exactly like my habit of walking or of writing; it is lived and acted, rather than re-presented.'[5] He maintained that our present moment of embodied experience is both sensation – a memory as perception of the immediate past – and movement: an action as determination of the immediate future. Intriguingly, he described experience as a 'section' in which the body stands:

> in that continuity of becoming which is reality itself, the present moment is constituted by the quasi-instantaneous section effected by our perception in the flowing mass, and this section is precisely that which we call the material world. Our body occupies its center.

Bergson noted that lived experience is defined by both 'affectivity and memory', indicating that embodiment could also take the form of being emotionally moved or affected by the mood of a space that one inhabits: 'Into our perception, then, something of our body must enter.'[6]

Bergson's theme of the embodiment of experience and memory is taken up by the philosopher Edward S. Casey in his 1987 book *Remembering: A Phenomenological Study*, where he states: 'there is no memory without body memory.'[7] Casey begins his chapter on 'Place Memory' with an epigraph drawn from the writings of Edmund Husserl:

> In this unique world, everything that I now originally perceive, everything that I have perceived and which I can now remember or about which others can report to me as what they perceived or remembered, has a place.[8]

Casey traces the understanding of emplaced memory to the ancient Greeks, who believed that while time was inherently dispersive, place was inherently collective or aggregative, and that in the Greek 'art of memory . . . the role of place was altogether central'. Casey quotes Aristotle's definition: 'Place is thought to be a kind of surface and as it were a vessel, i.e. a container' and notes that, while human action and experience is transitory, 'It is the stabilizing persistence of place as a container of experiences that contributes so powerfully to its intrinsic memorability.'[9]

Beyond the fundamental ways in which occupants orient themselves in place – up–down, front–back, left–right – Casey defined 'in-habitation', the *habitual* way of being *in* a place, as 'the manner in which, thanks precisely to the lived body, we find ourselves to be *familiar* with a particular place *in* which we are located'. This is related to 'appropriating' place, or making a place one's own in experience and memory, and Casey notes 'the exceedingly close tie between body memory and place memory – close to the point of their becoming virtually indistinguishable in many lived experiences of remembering.' To feel at home is to in-habit, he writes: 'In-habitation, we may conclude, is at once an effectuation and culmination of bodily being-in-place.' Paralleling Appleton's landscape experience attributes of prospect and refuge, Casey maintains that 'aspects of place in its *landscape* character' affect the sensory experience and body memory of place: 'Thanks precisely to our body as a basis of orientation, we find ourselves surrounded by a horizon, whatever our immediate location may be.' Casey concludes his chapter on place memory by stating:

Memory of place emplaces us and thus empowers us: gives us space to *be* precisely because *we have been* in so many memorable places . . . If body memory moves us – it is the prime mover of our memorial lives – it moves us directly into place, whose very immobility contributes to its distinct potency in matters of memory.[10]

In exploring the way in which lived experiences and recollected memories are most movingly and lastingly embodied within rooms conceived as places of inhabitation, we turn first to Modern rooms that provide their inhabitants with a simultaneous sense of extending out to connect to the distant horizon and withdrawing into close places of repose. In the engagement of prospect and refuge, three types of interior spaces may be discerned in Modern buildings, the first responding most directly to the dramatically increased employment of large sheets of transparent glass in the Modern period. Wright, whose own use of glass tended to the production of fine-grained woven and patterned windows as 'shimmering fabrics', noted in 1928: 'Perhaps the greatest difference eventually between ancient and modern buildings will be due to our modern machine-made glass,' and that, because of the availability of large sheets of inexpensive glass, 'our modern world is drifting towards structures of glass and steel' – a prospect about which Wright was ambivalent, noting: 'Glass and light [are] two forms of the same thing,' and yet the ability to form 'the space within' depended on precisely how glass was used."

The most notable type of glass-enabled interior space is the Modern all-glass building, which, due to the complete transparency of the bounding walls, may be defined as 'all prospect and no refuge', or, alternatively, as the prospect of the inhabitant across the landscape of the building becoming their refuge. Such an exposure of refuge to view is only possible if the entire landscape within visual range of the building belongs to the building as a private realm. The canonical example of this type is Mies van der Rohe's Farnsworth House, built on a large site on the Fox River in Illinois in 1950. The inhabitant may be said to enter the house the moment it comes into view, for its all-glass exterior walls allow the eye to look right through to the trees beyond. The floors, stairs and ceiling are all thin horizontal planes separated by air, floating above the landscape surrounding the house, which becomes the larger 'interior' room in experience when one recognizes that the floor, which is elevated above the landscape, aligns precisely with the horizon line – with one's eye-level. Upon entering the house, the primary vista or prospect is out towards the river to the south, off the surface of which the sun is reflected. One is effectively given refuge in the extensive prospect across the river, forest and field, and in inhabiting the house, one is seen by those outside to be standing on the horizon line.

The second Modern building type is that which engages prospect and refuge in an equal manner, and in the expression of this 'balanced prospect and refuge' character the canonical example is Wright's Fallingwater, or Kaufmann House, built above a small waterfall in a forest in Pennsylvania in 1938. The house is a balanced composition of vertical stone walls and horizontal concrete floor planes cantilevered out into space and interlaced with glass. From within the deeply shadowed refuge of the interior, one's view is not of the waterfall below but of the canopies of the surrounding trees. The writer and literary critic Robert Pogue Harrison, in his *Forests: Shadows of Civilization* (1992), notes:

> the surrounding forest seems to gather around the lateral
> extension of the house and to become more itself in its
> presence, as if the house had somehow elevated the earth
> to the height of the leaves in order to dramatize its reality
> as the ground that supports both forest and house.

Harrison traces Wright's inspiration to Henry David Thoreau's *Walden*, one of Wright's favourite books, observing:

> what is most reminiscent of *Walden* is the way the house exploits
> the dynamic relation between the flowing water and solid
> foundations. Thoreau did not want to drift on the streams
> of convention. He did not want to live in a houseboat but
> in a house built on the foundations of reality, on the earth.

For Harrison, Fallingwater is such a reality: '[It] is a masterpiece of stability: a solidity that stabilizes the various elements of the environment by virtue of its repose on the earth. Such a house makes its dwelling place the space of freedom.'[12]

Harrison notes Wright's connection of the horizon line, as it is perceived from the space within, with freedom:

> The search for freedom in horizontality, and not in the celestial nostalgias of the vertical rise, makes of Wright an American in the exceptional, Thoreauvian sense. Whatever freedom we may call ours is to be found on the earth . . . For those *on* the earth its surface extends horizontally, that is to say, constitutes a horizon. A house is that which gathers the horizon around itself.

Harrison points out that Wright defined shelter as 'vista within and vista without', as broad openness to the surrounding landscape from within the protected interior, rather than as complete closure. 'The only true shelter on earth is the earth itself,' yet the earth has 'a natural tendency to draw back into its absolute closure'. Harrison notes Wright's definition of the architecture of dwelling as 'unfolding' rather than 'enfolding', and he goes on to maintain that the lesson of Fallingwater is that 'the earth cannot become a shelter unless it is unfolded, or disclosed, by human appropriation . . . the disclosure of freedom in the space of dwelling.'[13]

The third Modern interpretation are the buildings which, due to the almost complete translucency or opacity of the bounding walls, may be defined as 'all refuge and no prospect', or, alternatively, as the prospect being directed inward towards the refuge so that the vista without *is* the vista within. This introspective interior interpretation appeared at the very beginning of Modern architecture, in the work of Adolf Loos. This aspect of Loos's work was first pointed out by none other than Le Corbusier, who in his *Urbanisme* of 1925 wrote: 'Loos told me one day: "A cultivated man does not look out of the window; his windows are ground glass; it is there only to let light in, not to let the gaze pass through.'"[14] The architectural historian Beatriz Colomina notes this generally overlooked feature of Loos's houses:

> not only are the windows either [translucent] or covered with sheer curtains, but the organization of the spaces and the disposition of the built-in furniture . . . seem to hinder access to them. A sofa is often placed at the foot of a window so as to position the occupants with their back to it, facing the room . . . Moreover, upon entering a Loos interior one's body is continually turned around to face the space one has just moved through, rather than the upcoming space [in the movement sequence] or the space outside.[15]

The most remarkable example of this 'all refuge and no prospect' type of interior is in fact built almost entirely of glass: Pierre Chareau's Maison de Verre (House of Glass), the Dalsace Residence in Paris (1932). The interior of the house is experienced as a 'cave of glass', its exterior walls built almost entirely of translucent glass blocks so that the open interior space is a refuge enclosed by luminous walls, paradoxically flooded with light while being given only the most minimal prospect to the outside. The vista within is composed of thin layers of solid materials, all of which are eroded by light, as occurs in the separation into floating planes of the entry stairs, or the perforation of the metal screens and doors, or the levitation and activation of almost all of the components shaping the space within the house. Almost everything in the house appears to be set in motion — pivoting, folding, hovering, hinging or

The new gallery reiterates the character of natural light, colour and proportion of the studio in which works on display were made, the memory of both binding the two rooms together in experience. Carlo Scarpa, Gipsoteca Canoviana, Possagno, Italy, interior view of main gallery, analysis of gallery and Canova studio; sketch made on 4 September 2004.

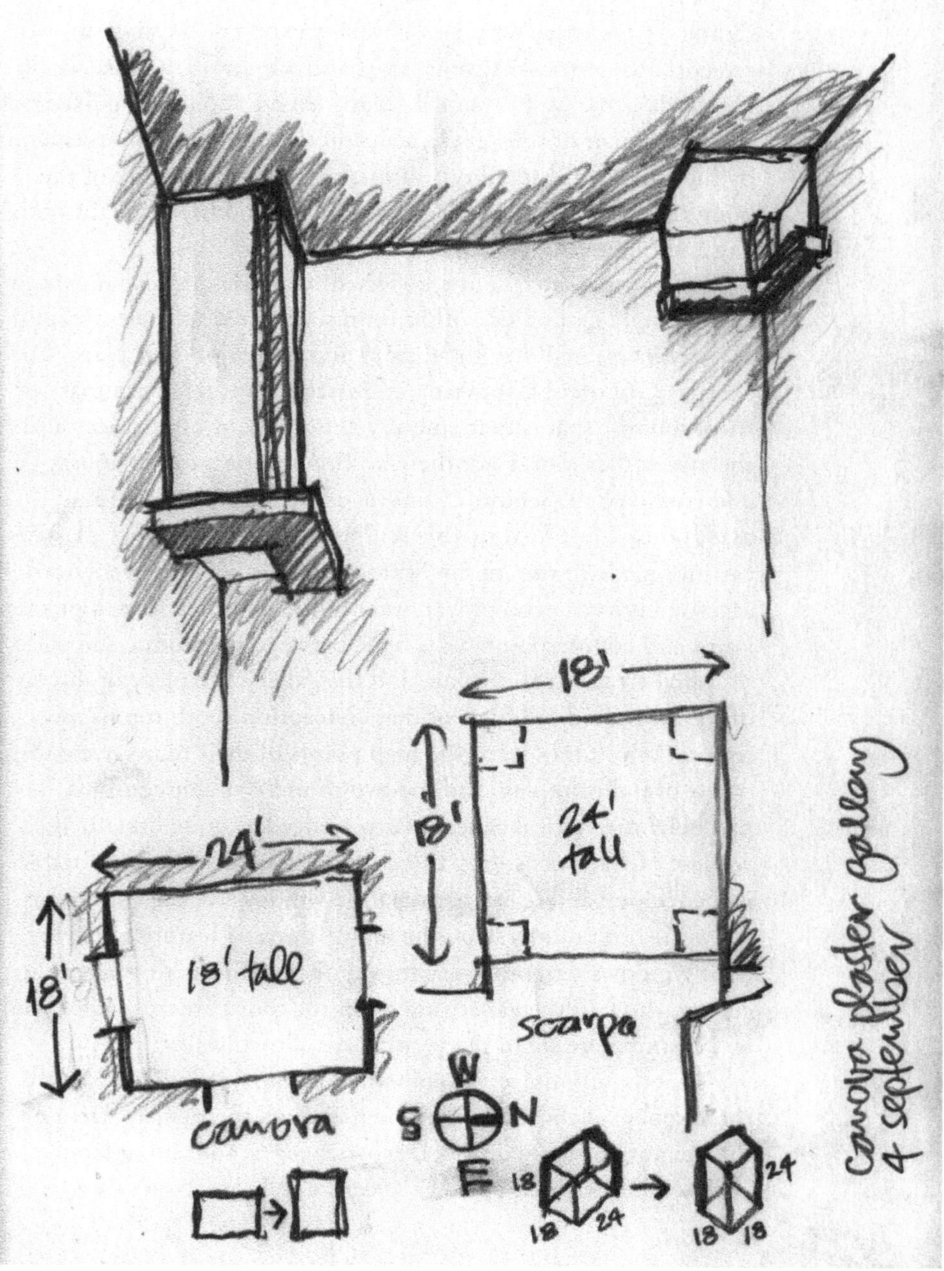
24'
18'
18' tall
camera
18'
24'
24' tall
scarpa
W
S N
E
18
18 24
24
18 18
Canova Plaster Gallery
4 september

sliding – from those we might normally expect to do so, such as the screens, cabinets, doors, ventilators and windows, to those we do not, such as the walls, stairs, beds and even the plumbing fixtures. The movement of smaller elements on the interior is complemented by the paradoxical stability and thick massive luminosity of the bounding glass-block walls, glowing all around us with light both day and night.

Lived experiences and recollected memories are also movingly and lastingly embodied within rooms anchored to their sites and thereby integrated into the history and nature of their place. Carlo Scarpa's Gipsoteca Canoviana in Possagno (1957) is exemplary of these interior spaces that embody a memory of built places and the events that took place therein. This addition to the house and studio of the sculptor Canova, as well as to a museum of 1836, housed not final marble sculptures but preparatory plaster castings made in the studio. Scarpa's taller gallery is experienced as an intentional echo of Canova's studio, and they form a precise point and counterpoint, a dialogue between the studio, the place of initial creative conception, and the gallery, the place of display of the fabricated products of that conception. Both rooms are tower-like volumes set at the high points of their respective ends of the overall complex, and the two rooms share dimensions – precisely: the vertical gallery is experienced as quite literally the volume of Canova's studio tilted up on its end. Most memorable is the reciprocal relation between the windows in the two rooms, for while both rooms share the highly unusual feature of having their windows set at the very tops of their walls, hard against the ceiling, those in the gallery are set in the four corners, while those in the studio are set in the very centre of each wall.

In counterpoint to the embodied memory of built places are those rooms anchored to their sites through their engagement of the memory of natural places, experienced as an echo of landscape enclosed inside the room. At the centre of Jørn Utzon's Bagsværd

Church in Denmark (1976) is a room that recollects and transforms the memory of the landscape as the place of dwelling, on the earth and under the sky. Appearing from outside as a quiet, rectangular enclosure, reminding one of agricultural buildings, the shell-like exterior conceals the space within. Entering through the top-lit peripheral hallway, a kind of inverted cloister walk, one arrives into the main sanctuary, a large room dominated by a hovering white concrete ceiling that is lit by hidden clerestory windows at the top of its sensuous curves. The ceiling runs across the room from left to right and rhythmically rises towards heaven and swoops back down over our heads as it unfurls from the altar at the front to the entry court at back. Suffused with an ethereal light, the billowing, curving ceiling recalls the characteristically low-hanging clouds outside, while the horizontal tile floor recalls the flat landscape of Danish countryside that surrounds us. Experienced together, the floor and ceiling place the inhabitant between earth and sky.

Lived experiences and recollected memories are also embodied within rooms resonant with the memory of their making, legible in their structure, materials and joinery. The Bruder Klaus Field Chapel (2007) near Wachendorf, Germany, by Peter Zumthor is a small concrete tower standing in an agricultural landscape. The scale of the five-sided chapel is hard to determine until one is actually close to it, as the exterior is marked only by the subtle horizontal lines between the 24 layers of rammed concrete, each 50 cm deep, poured in a day and punctured by widely spaced small holes, which permanently record the time of construction. A triangular metal door, larger below and tapering to a point above, leads into the curving interior. The narrow, confining interior space, matte black and irregularly shaped, curves away from view – then we become aware of the strong smell of smoke. Daylight from the small opening at the top dimly illuminates the rough repetitive vertical concavities of the surrounding walls. We slowly come to realize that we are standing in a space formed by 112 tree trunks arranged in a tent-like configuration, around which concrete was poured, and after which the tree trunks were burned out, leaving their curved imprint, black soot and smoke smell. The rough, vertically striated darkness of the interior is punctuated by the daylight coming through dozens of small glass elements set into the cylindrical holes cast into the wall.

Lived experiences and recollected memories are also embodied within rooms brought to life by the play of light throughout the day, the season and the year. Louis Kahn, the foremost Modern exponent of natural light, said:

> We are born of light. The seasons are felt through light. We only know the world as it is evoked by light . . . To me natural light is the only light, because it has mood – it provides a ground of common agreement for man – it puts us in touch with the eternal.[16]

Paraphrasing the American poet Wallace Stevens, Kahn said: 'A great American poet once asked the architect, "What slice of sun does your building have? What light enters your room?"'[17] The experiences of rooms in Kahn's buildings are predominantly embodied in the individual's interactions with natural light. Upon entering Exeter Library, we rise up into a great room at the building's centre, where we see all the books through monumentally scaled concrete circular openings. Then, after finding our book, we 'take the book to the light', as Kahn said, reading the book in natural light, sitting in intimately scaled wooden carrels housed in the folds of the masonry construction at the building's outer edges. In counterpoint, the experience of Kahn's Kimbell Art Museum (1972) in Fort Worth, Texas, is one in which we move through a series of rooms formed not by walls but by extended concrete vaults overhead, each of which paradoxically both shades the interior from the hot sun and gives it light. Each vault is split down the centre by a line of light that is bounced up onto the curved underside of the vaults, illuminating the rooms with a light that is at once consistently ethereal and continually changing with the passing of each cloud.

Finally, lived experiences and recollected memories are also embodied within rooms tailored precisely to the rituals of daily life that take place within them. In counterpoint to Loos's inward focus, in the early houses of Le Corbusier, the rituals of living are opened and oriented to the landscape outside. In the Villa Savoye, the top-lit master bathroom – the only room that does not touch the outer wall – is separated from but also connected to the master bedroom by a tiled chaise longue at the edge of the bath, from which the inhabitant can look out the continuous horizontal window into the forest. In what Le Corbusier called the *petite maison* designed for his parents on Lake Geneva in 1925, the rooms within the house are lined up between the closed wall to the road behind and a continuous horizontal window to the front, providing an expansive view of the mountains across the lake. Yet when designing the small garden at one end of the house, a space that is actually an exterior, he built tall masonry walls to enclose the space and make it a room:

> The object of the wall . . . is to block off the view . . . for the ever-present view and overpowering scenery on all sides has a tiring effect in the long run . . . To lend significance to the scenery one has to restrict and give it proportion; the view must be blocked by walls that are only pierced at certain strategic points and there permit an unhindered view.[18]

The *petite maison's* garden room's single view of the mountains and lake was framed by a small, square opening into the sill of which a table was built, which was where Le Corbusier had dinner with his mother after his father passed away.

In their recognition of the primacy of the experience of the interior room, and its importance as the setting for the daily rituals and events of life, Modern architects are paralleled by writers, who present a very different interpretation of interior space than that typically given by architectural history and criticism. In her book *The Sense of an Interior*, a study of Dickinson, Freud, Keller and Proust and 'the rooms that shaped them', the literary critic Diana Fuss begins by noting:

> Few architectural studies explore how specific individuals creatively dwell in their houses. Architectural criticism focuses attention instead on the overall built environment, evacuating the house of its inhabitants . . . the prevailing tendency in architecture is to study only the many different ways a habitation might be built, not the many different ways it might be occupied.

In her study of Marcel Proust and his novel sequence *À la recherche du temps perdu*, Fuss notes that the book is 'as much a book about the search for lost space as the search for lost time'. She begins by noting:

> Perhaps no writer describes better the sense of a room – its sights, sounds, odors and textures – than Marcel Proust . . . That Proust is a writer of the interior quite nearly goes without saying; we might readily define this most influential of French modernists in terms Proust himself uses to describe his narrator, a writer who works 'from the inside outwards.'

Fuss goes on to note that *À la recherche du temps perdu*, written in Proust's bedroom and largely concerned with experiences and memories of a writer and the rooms he inhabits, was praised as a definitive statement regarding modern life by Benjamin, Bergson and Hannah Arendt, among others.[19]

In the literary critic Marilyn Chandler's *Dwelling in the Text*, a study of houses and their interior rooms in the American fiction of Thoreau, Poe, Hawthorne, James, Wharton, Cather, Fitzgerald and Faulkner, among others, she observes the powerful shaping effect on the experience of the people that inhabit the rooms described in the novels. In her study of Thoreau's *Walden*, the story of the Transcendentalist writer's construction and inhabitation of a one-room house in the woods on Walden Pond, Massachusetts, Chandler notes that Thoreau, who so strongly influenced Modern architects such as Wright and Kahn, felt one of the only drawbacks to his small, ascetic house was the lack of the space necessary for dialogue to unfold between inhabitants. Thoreau wrote:

> One inconvenience I sometimes experienced in so small a house, the difficulty of getting a sufficient distance from my guest when we began to utter the big thoughts in big words. You want room for your thoughts to get to sailing trim and run a course or two before they make their port . . . Our sentences wanted room to unfold . . . As the conversation began to assume a loftier and grander tone, we gradually shoved our chairs farther apart till they touched the wall in opposite corners, and then commonly there was not room enough.

This idea that different rooms engender different kinds of thought and behaviour in their occupants would be later reprised in many of the lectures of Louis Kahn. In her study of Edith Wharton, Chandler concludes:

> The relationship of character to environment is emphatically reciprocal, and the houses the characters inhabit influence them as these houses reflect the characters' influence . . . We are, Wharton seems to suggest, increasingly dependent on the environments we create around ourselves, so that finally they

form us, and what we are becomes inseparably a function of where and how we live.[20]

In the novel *The Notebook of Malte Laurids Brigge* (1910), the poet Rainer Maria Rilke gave some of the most vivid descriptions of the way interior space embedded itself in the experience and memory of the modern inhabitant. In recalling his grandfather's house, the narrator says:

It is not a complete building; it is all broken up in my memory, a room here, and a room there, and then part of a hallway that does not connect these two rooms but is preserved as a fragment in itself. In this way it is all dispersed within me – the rooms, the stairways that descended with such ceremonious deliberation, and the other narrow, spiral stairs in the obscurity of which one moved as blood does in the veins . . . all this is still inside me and will never cease to be in me. It is as though the picture of this house had fallen into me from an immeasurable height, and had been shattered on my innermost being.

Later, in describing the party walls of a demolished apartment building in the same neighbourhood, Rilke wrote:

But the walls themselves were the most unforgettable. The stubborn life of these rooms had not allowed itself to be trampled out. It was still there; it clung to the nails that had been left in the walls; it found a resting-place on the remaining handsbreadth of flooring; it squatted beneath the corner beams where a little bit of space remained.[21]

In Simon Mawer's novel *The Glass Room*, the Modern glass house, based directly on Mies van der Rohe's Villa Tugendhat in Brno (1930), is as much a character in the novel as the people who inhabit it. In the opening scene, the now blind owner returns to visit the house she had abandoned thirty years before when the city was overrun in the war, and she recalls the experience of the space:

> Sounds, the mere whisper of hearing, gave her the dimensions of the space . . . She could feel the volume as though it had physical substance, as though her face were immersed in it. Space made manifest. She could feel the light from the expanse of plate glass that made up the south wall, smell the Macassar wood, sense the people standing there between the glass and the onyx wall, between the plain white ceiling and the ivory white floor . . . Snow. Why did she think of snow? That particular bath of light, the sky's light reflected upwards from the blanched lawn to light the ceiling as brightly as the clouded sun lit the floor. Light became substance, soft transparent milk.

At the end of the novel, another person who lived in the house visits again after more than fifty years, experiencing 'the Glass Room [as] an ageless place held in a rectilinear frame that handles light like a substance and volume like a tangible material and denies the very existence of time'.[22]

The characters in Mawer's novel quote from another novel of the period, *Nadja* (1928) by the Surrealist writer André Breton, in which a romance unfolds in the context of emerging Modernism in all the arts. Immediately before commenting on his friend Tristan Tzara (whose solid-walled Paris house was designed by Adolf Loos), the narrator enumerates the benefits of his Modern glass house:

> I myself shall continue living in my glass house where you can always see who comes to call; where everything hanging from the ceiling and from the walls stays there as if by magic, where I sleep nights in a glass bed, under glass sheets, and where *who I am* will sooner or later appear etched by a diamond.[23]

The Italian writer Curzio Malaparte, after first cooperating with
and then criticizing the Fascist regime in Italy, was imprisoned on
the island of Lipari, an experience he later described:

> Today more than ever I feel that cell number 461 . . . has remained
> inside me, becoming the secret of my soul. Today more than ever,
> I feel like a bird that has swallowed his cage. I take my cell with
> me, as a pregnant woman carries her baby in her womb.[24]

Upon returning to Italy, Malaparte (with the assistance in the early
stages of the architect Adalberto Libera) developed the design and
directed the construction of a house of unprecedented form that
incorporated both the enclosure of his prison cell and the triangular
staircase rising to the small church of the Annunziata on Lipari.
The house, which Malaparte called Casa Come Me (House Like
Me) and said was a 'ritratto di pietra' (self-portrait in stone), is sited
on a rocky promontory projecting into the Mediterranean on the
island of Capri. Entry requires ascending a massive staircase that
climbs to a roof plaza in the sky, and once inside the main room of
the house, one finds four large windows opened in the walls, giving
views of the cliffs and sea below, and another window opened in the
rear of the fireplace, providing a light for the boats to avoid running
aground. In Malaparte's semi-autobiographical novel *The Skin* (1947),
the narrator describes a visit by the German field marshal Rommel
to his house, the Villa Malaparte:

> I accompanied him all over the house, going from room to room
> . . . and when we returned to the vast hall with its great windows,
> which look out onto the most beautiful scenery in the world,
> I offered him a glass of Vesuvian wine . . . Then, before leaving,
> he asked me whether I bought my house as it stood or whether
> I designed and built it myself. I replied – and it was not true
> – that I had bought the house as it stood. And with a sweeping

gesture, indicating the sheer cliff of Matromania, the three gigantic rocks of Faraglioni, the peninsula of Sorrento, the islands of the Sirens, the far away blue coastline of Amalfi, and the golden sands of Paestum, shimmering in the distance, I said to him: 'I designed the scenery.'[25]

On the otherwise closed side of the building, an intimate space folded out of the wall, with a sky window lighting the space carved from the thickness of the wall, existing between outside and inside. Alvar Aalto, Studio Aalto, Tiilimäki, Helsinki, Finland, interior view of top-lighted display wall in conference room, facing street, with plan and section; sketch made on 14 March 2007.

Nine

Interior Experience of the Exterior Environment

It may seem paradoxical at first mention, but the interior experience of the exterior environment is a critical aspect of this conception of interior primacy in architecture. Architects whose interior spaces remain in our memory have invariably been acutely sensitive to the local climate, the constant change of the seasons and natural light, and the larger environment in which the building is placed, and how these may be engaged to enrich the experience of the inhabitants in the space within. Aldo van Eyck believed that all inhabited rooms – even exterior rooms such as urban squares – are fundamentally interiors, and held that all spaces designed by mankind, inside or outside, rooms or streets, must be fundamentally conceived and experienced as interior spaces. Architecture that lasts involves the construction of interior space that is grounded in its place, that uses minimal resources and has minimal impact on the environment, and that provides maximal engagement of its environment and maximal enrichment of experience for its inhabitants.

Yet it is important to recognize that the vast majority of buildings constructed around the world in the last sixty years have been designed to address another paradigm – the uniform mechanical heating and cooling of all interior spaces. Without question, the now virtually universal mechanical air-conditioning of interior spaces – the hermetic sealing of buildings which cuts the occupants off from any contact (other than visual, through glass windows) with their climate and environment – has led to a steady erosion of our perceived need for protective and porous layers of construction, materials that are appropriately warm or cool to the touch, depending on the season, and the intimate scale of furnishings in our architecture. We can trace a direct path from the time when human comfort depended on the intimate layer of architecture – such as St Jerome's wooden study – to the time when human comfort became almost entirely independent of it, reliant instead on the thermostat regulating the hermetically sealed interior. That this cutting off of the inside from the larger outside occurred simultaneously with the rise of the profession of 'interior design' and the definition of architecture as being concerned only with 'the last six inches' – the building skin and the exterior form – is hardly coincidental.

The mechanical air-conditioning of hermetically sealed interior spaces has been paralleled by two related practices that are equally destructive of the relation of interior experience to exterior environment: the flattening and re-grading of existing natural topography in order to accept the construction of pre-determined and non-site-specific floor plans, and the removal of indigenous trees and vegetation and their replacement with non-native decorative 'landscaping', which almost inevitably accompanies it. These have been paralleled by the disappearance of locally sourced building materials and regional traditions of building, and their replacement by universally available prefabricated materials and assembly systems, which has in turn made possible the rise of de-contextualized and de-natured architectural 'styles' intended to house a so-called 'globalized' lifestyle. These buildings could in fact be constructed anywhere, and thus those inhabiting them are, quite literally, nowhere. Van Eyck argued that the worst damage done to the daily lives of people by Modern society was the result of 'its capacity to create "nowhere" everywhere'.[1] Even more deleterious than the fact that these buildings are not ecologically 'sustainable' by any definition of the word is the way they deny the unfortunate occupants of their interiors any sensory engagement with the exterior environments that lie just outside their glass windows.

However, the recent emphasis on what is today called 'sustainable' or 'green' construction – really a renewal or rediscovery, because it is a way of building that is as old as architecture and human dwelling itself – is beginning to erode this universal commitment to mechanical air-conditioning. As a result, the best architecture being realized today re-establishes the paradigms, inherent in ancient ways of building, of minimal energy use, employment of recycled and renewable materials, maintaining ecological balance, passive tempering of climate, appropriate infusion of daylight into the interior, minimal impact on the environment and maximal experiential engagement of its exterior place.

Before air conditioning, uniformly flat site grading, 'landscaping' and universal building systems and materials together made all places and climates alike and separated interior inhabitants from their place in the exterior natural world, architects had no choice but to engage their climate and natural context. This was an environmental imperative, in response to which early Modern architects tended to engage the local traditions of ecologically appropriate building. In this effort, both the vernacular and the work of predecessors was critical to learning methods of design and construction that would last, as well as techniques for the appropriate engagement of climate. The majority of early Modern architecture was built largely before air conditioning, and its architects of necessity employed such place-determining and experientially beneficial aspects as solar orientation, tree shading and prevailing breezes, as well as the smells of the forest after a rain and the sounds of native bird calls – nestling their buildings into their sites and adjusting them to its nature. This sense of natural economy as an ethic of building – gaining the maximum benefit for the inhabitants of its interiors, in terms of the enrichment of the daily rituals of life over the lifetime of a building, from the least energy and material investment – has always been part of Modern architecture that has lasted.

The ideal of intertwining the architectural interior, and the life that takes place in the space within, with the exterior environment in which it was built, was part of Modern architecture from the very start. One of the primary themes of Modern architecture, articulated at its beginning by Wright, is bringing the outside in, and extending the inside out: 'We have no longer an outside and an inside as two separate things. Now the outside may come inside, and the inside may and does go outside. They are of each other.'[2] Wright believed that daily life should take place in the presence of nature, which should be an integral part of the interior experience:

> Buildings perform their highest function in relation to human life within and the natural efflorescence without; and to develop and maintain the harmony for a true chord between them, making the building in this sense a sure foil for life.[3]

In designing his houses, Wright gave the entire site a geometric order: the low walls, terraces, stairs, piers and planters anchored the house to the earth, projecting the spatial grid of the house out into the landscape and simultaneously pulling the landscape into the house: 'Intimate harmony was thus established not only in the house but with its site.'[4] He took great care to assure that the spaces within his houses were oriented to receive sun at appropriate times during the day:

> Proper orientation of the house, then, is the first condition of the lighting of that house . . . The sun is the great luminary of all life. It should serve as such in the building of any house.[5]

Wright's interior spaces allowed the inhabitants to experience the close relationship between architecture (to build and edify) and

School forming a new porous city wall at the edge of the town, with passage from urban plaza to natural forest crossed by extended loggia, allowing students to be at once inside and outside. Mario Botta. Morbio Inferiore secondary school, Switzerland, view of loggia; sketch made on 24 September 2004.

agriculture (to care for and cultivate the land) as related ways of tending and transforming the landscape. In describing what he called 'the natural house', Wright emphasized the importance of integrating the interior of the house with the exterior garden. In this the architect should 'make the garden be the building as much as the building will be the garden, the sky as treasured a feature of daily indoor life as the ground itself'.[6] In Wright's Usonian houses, the garden takes up the geometric centre of both the actual site and the plan drawing, and is the focus of the entire spatial composition. Examination of the paired perspectives Wright drew of a prototypical Usonian house of 1935 reveals the reading of 'inside' and 'outside' he intended for the site itself. The street view is depicted from an elevated viewpoint, off the ground, indicating that we are outside the habitable realm of the house, looking at a closed object in the landscape. Compare this to the matched garden view, depicted from eye-level on the ground, where we feel as if we are standing in the garden itself, enclosed by the wings of the open house. We are in the most important room of the house: the garden.

This orientation to the garden, as the centre of the house and the life that goes on within it, is complemented by Wright's insistence on the proper solar orientation for the primary glazed elevations facing the garden – southeast, south or southwest. Wright was so adamant about this aspect that he advised clients to seek his approval prior to purchasing a building plot, so that he could assure that the house would have the correct orientation for the sun. This insistence on proper orientation benefited both the energy use (the practical function) and the life lived 'in the sunlight' (the poetic function). It comes as no surprise that Wright was adamantly opposed to both the flattening of landscape contours and the mechanical control of climate:

> To me air conditioning is a dangerous circumstance . . . I think it far better to go with the natural climate than to try to fix a special

artificial climate of your own. Climate means something to man. It means something in relations to one's life in it.[7]

Wright also opposed the disregard for the character of the landscape that came with speculative development: 'Architecture and its kindred, as a matter of course, are divorced from nature in order to make of [architecture] the merchantable thing . . . It is a speculative commodity.'[8] Instead, he argued for integrity of design and an integration of exterior environment and interior experience: 'The Usonian house, then, aims to be a natural performance, one that is integral to site, integral to environment, integral to the life of the inhabitants.'[9]

A conceptual chasm separates our time from the time when Wright began his career by apprenticing in the office of Adler & Sullivan rather than attending university, learning through making in what may be called 'the tradition of practice': a fully integrated experience binding all principles of the ethical practice of architecture – the economic, functional, ecological, constructive, structural, material, aesthetic, sensorial, social and cultural aspects that together affect our experience of inhabitation of the space within, which remains the ultimate measure of a work of architecture. The architecture made by those engaged in the tradition of practice is invariably characterized by a combination of the practical and the poetic. The practical engages the aspects of appropriateness, functional suitability, economy in the limited use of energy and resources, proper solar orientation and local material culture. On the other hand, the poetic involves the efforts to enrich the experience of the inhabitants through the engagement of local climate, context and culture, understanding that architecture is where life quite literally takes place. When Wright began his practice, only the poetic qualities of an architect's work were considered worth presenting to clients as arguments for being selected as their architect. This was because, for those engaged in the tradition of practice, the practical aspects of architectural practice were considered the absolute minimum definition of professional competence, and thus were not worth mentioning; if someone did not take care of the practical matters in their first design, they would simply not receive a second commission, and would need to find another profession.

The degree to which Wright's integrated understanding of architecture and environment had disappeared from professional practices only ten years after his death was indicated when, in 1969, Reyner Banham astonished almost all in the profession when he noted, among other innovative environmental tempering features of the Robie House of 1909, that the south roof overhangs shaded the glazed doors running along that side of the house with a level of precision shocking to those who assumed that energy-efficiency had only much more recently been discovered as a determinant of architectural form. He pointed out that at noon on the summer solstice, the longest day of the year, the roof overhang on the south side 'is *exactly* sufficient . . . the shadow of the eaves just kisses the woodwork at the bottom of the glass in the doors of the terrace'.[10] We should also note that in thus shading the south glass, the overhangs at the Robie House do not lose any of the spatial dynamism and sculptural beauty of line that had heretofore been regarded as their (purely) formal determinants. Both intentions, today invariably assumed to be mutually exclusive, are simultaneously accomplished in this product of Wright's integrated practice, rendering the more practical intention (shading of glass) unremarkable, while rendering the more poetic aspect (plastic expression of cantilever in space) remarkable. Banham went on to enumerate a series of what we today call 'passive' – requiring no energy expenditure – environmental tempering devices, such as the oversized chimney that acts as a flue to exhaust hot air, including that generated by recessed lighting, out of the house. What Banham did not note, but which can be experienced by anyone inhabiting the Robie House at noon on the winter solstice, the shortest day of the year, is that the same roof overhang along the south side of the house that shades so precisely in summer allows the low winter sun to reach all the way across the living and dining rooms to 'just kiss' the base of the north wall, so that the sun warms the entire width of the concrete floor slab.

In *Art as Experience*, John Dewey argued that the initial impulse to build and make is inspired by 'the loss of integration with the environment' and desire for the recovery of that union. He maintained, similarly to Bergson, that

> We unconsciously carry over this belief in the bounded character of all *objects* of experience . . . into our conception of experience itself. We suppose the experience has the same definite limits as the things with which it is concerned. But any experience the most ordinary, has an indefinite total setting . . . the sense, the feeling of unlimited envelope becomes intense . . . For although there is a bounding horizon, it moves as we move.

Dewey criticizes the idea that anything of the character or essence of experience can be captured by a photograph: 'An instantaneous experience is an impossibility, biologically and psychologically.' Indeed, owing to the durability of architecture and its engagement of nature, through its being constructed of natural materials, 'buildings, among all art objects, come the nearest to expressing the stability and endurance of existence.' In what could be interpreted as a description of a house designed by Wright, with its massive central hearth, interweaving perimeter walls and over-hanging roof eaves, all enclosing the inhabitant in ambiguous boundary layers, Dewey wrote:

> Through going out into the environment, position unfolds into volume; through the pressure of environment, mass is retracted

into energy of position, and space remains, when matter
is contracted, as an opportunity for further action.[11]

In the essay 'The Dialectics of Outside and Inside', which closes
his book *The Poetics of Space*, Bachelard argues against either the
binary opposition or reciprocity of interior and exterior as they
are applied to spatial experience and the poetics of space,
calling instead for a more intertwined understanding of these
complementary concepts:

In any case, inside and outside, as experienced . . . can no longer
be taken in their simple reciprocity; consequently, by omitting
geometrical references when we speak of the first expressions of
being, by choosing more concrete, more phenomenologically
exact inceptions, we shall come to realize that the dialectics of
inside and outside multiply with countless diversified nuances.[12]

Bachelard's arguments serve to remind us that we cannot experience
interiority except against the complementary space of exteriority,
and that architecture engenders and embodies experience through
the provision of a layered overlapping of interior space and exterior
environment, in which we can inhabit thick walls, window seats,
porches and covered terraces.

During the period when he was transitioning from his classical
academic education to his Modern practice, Alvar Aalto wrote
a series of articles for Finnish newspapers and journals, and one
of the most important for his later career defined the importance
of the space between the interior and exterior. In a 1926 commentary
on Fra Angelico's *The Annunciation*, titled 'From Doorstep to Living
Room', Aalto interpreted the painting as showing an interplay
between interior and exterior space, emphasizing the human action,
the experience of stepping into a room, rather than the form of the
door itself:

The picture provides an ideal example of 'entering a room'. The trinity of *human being, room and garden* shown in the picture make it an unattainable ideal image of the home . . . Two things stand out plainly: the unity of the room, the external wall, and the garden, and the formation of these elements so as to give the human figure prominence and express her state of mind . . . The garden (or courtyard) belongs to the home just as much as any of the rooms.

Introducing a photograph of the covered terrace of Le Corbusier's Pavillon de l'Esprit Nouveau of the year before, Aalto asked: 'Is it a hall, beautifully open to the exterior . . . or is it a garden built into the house, a garden room?' Aalto then argued for the ideal of the central courtyard-hall, which, when spacious, well-lit and differing in scale from the other rooms, may bring '*the open air under the home roof* . . . this idea of *the hall as an open-air space* . . . a point of transition between "outdoors and indoors".'[13]

Aalto engaged this enlarged understanding of the relation between interior space and exterior environment at widely varying scales in his own work. Aalto's houses involved reinterpretations and extensions of traditional ways of living in the Nordic landscape, including the sauna, a tiny all-wooden space of complete darkness, filled with heat and smoke. Due to the impossibility of focused vision, the room is experienced only through peripheral vision, hearing, smell, taste and, most importantly, touch, so that the inhabitants' thoughts turn inwards to the rhythms of their own bodies – an experience that is complemented by periodic immersions in the frigid waters of a frozen lake just outside, within the infinite whiteness of the winter landscape.

Aalto also engaged the single-room Finnish farmhouse, which in the darkness of the Arctic winter forms an interior world within, scaled to span from the intimacies depicted in Akseli Gallen-Kallela's *First Lesson* of 1889, showing a child reading by the light of a small deep window cut through the thick log walls of her farmhouse, her book catching the window's cold, blue-white light while her father's face is illuminated by the faint reddish glow of a fire, to the immensity of the farmhouse's massive single room, the *tupa*, an all-wooden 'forest womb' anchored by the fireplace-stove-oven and enclosing all the spaces of domestic life, where the human body is precisely housed in the furniture and beds built into and folding out of the walls, floors and ceilings.

An indication of the subtle relation between the encompassing environment and the room within may be found in Aalto's criticism of the tubular-steel-framed furnishings designed by Marcel Breuer. After purchasing several of the chairs for his own apartment in 1928, Aalto experienced the way in which the metal frames conducted heat away from the body during the Nordic winter, resulting in discomfort for the occupant. This realization led to Aalto's own development of bent-wood-framed furnishings, leather-wrapped door handles and wood-wrapped steel columns.

The experience of the overlapping and interpenetration of interior space and exterior environment, and its relation to Modern architecture, has been extensively explored in the writings of the American architectural historian David Leatherbarrow. Regarding the three early conceptions of interior space examined earlier, he noted:

> Wright, Le Corbusier and Loos all proposed a de-compartment-alized spatiality . . . Each of these configurations is a means by which the room or building transcends itself into its vicinity; or, in reverse, the means by which the potentials of the vicinity enter into and qualify the building's several settings.[14]

Arguing against the interpretation of Modern space as 'flowing' freely between inside and outside, and thus blurring their very real differences, he wrote:

Modern architecture did not eliminate the separation between inside and outside, so that the space of the one could flow into the other; it made that separation much more subtle than it had been in previous architectures. Boundaries between spatial interiors and exteriors are not overcome with the adoption of the structural frame, but thickened.[15]

In his important study of the relation between landscape and architecture in Modernism, *Uncommon Ground*, Leatherbarrow maintained:

Built form and land form must be understood as two different things, even when they have been made to correspond. This contrast gives both amplitude and dramatic tension to the field of articulations within any given site.

While much has been made of Wright's 'breaking the box' and other ways Modern architecture removed the barriers between inside and outside space, Leatherbarrow noted:

The distinction between interior and exterior was not renounced by the removal of so many walls; it was refashioned by being extended, through the use of window walls, cantilevers, and projecting slabs, as well as devices for accelerating and modulating 'thermal passage' from terrace to room and room to terrace.

Leatherbarrow maintained that the interior space of architecture and the exterior space of the environment are not the same kind of space: 'Landscape and building can be joined only if they are distinct, interlocked only if separate, for only when they are different can they perform their roles *similarly*.' The thickening of the space of inhabitation between inside and outside, to be found in overlapping spaces such as window seats, porches, terraces and courtyards, results in a true fusion of interior and exterior:

> This makes it possible for people to live both inside and outside their houses, and also in the in-between areas, the transitions between the 'inside' and the 'outside' . . . the building's margins were designed to transform an entirely palpable ambient quality into its desired opposite: warm air was cooled in summer, in the winter the reverse. Likewise were both glare and darkness moderated. The walls of the building were instruments of intertwining, according to which rooms and [exterior] fields could supply what each other lacked, like the sort of fabric that allows your skin to breathe while keeping it warm.[16]

From the very start of his career, Le Corbusier had argued against the traditional separation of interior and exterior, stating in 1930:

> I perceive that the project we are designing is neither alone nor isolated; that the air around it constitutes other surfaces, other grounds, other ceilings . . . A project is not made only of itself: its surroundings exist. The surroundings envelope me in their totality as a room . . . the outside is always an inside.[17]

Beatriz Colomina has noted of Le Corbusier's statement: 'To say that "the exterior is always an interior" means that the interior is not simply the bounded territory defined by its opposition to the exterior. The exterior is "inscribed" in the dwelling.'[18] Later in life, while he was working on his various projects in India, Le Corbusier described the courtyard of an old Indian building with a view of a nearby dome: 'It is a very interesting *interior exterior*.'[19]

This idea of 'interior exterior' characterizes Le Corbusier's Curutchet House (1949) in La Plata, Argentina, where the house is set at the rear of a vertical courtyard centred on a large tree, and the medical office of the owner is placed along the street front and elevated one floor above the ground. One enters by passing beneath the office volume and into the courtyard, ascending a ramp to reach the house, after which one passes back across the courtyard on a bridge to reach the covered terrace on the roof of the office, opening to both the street and courtyard. In experience the interior rooms of domestic and work life are completely intertwined with the exterior space of the courtyard, as well as the park across the street. Juhani Pallasmaa described his visit to the house:

> The house is extraordinarily spatial; it is simultaneously above and below, in front and behind, to the left and to the right of the visitor, and it embraces you as 'a cradle,' to use the expression of Bachelard. It is a spatialized *mandala*. The three levels of floors, terraces, ramps and stairways surround a huge tree in the center of the house as its mythical primordial inhabitant. The house is located in a row of buildings facing a park, and it stretches towards this open space and the world beyond. As I returned back home on the other side of the world, I realized that my body scheme had been re-calibrated by the house. For weeks, I was experiencing gravity, horizontality, and the cardinal orientations through this metaphysical instrument on the far side of the globe.[20]

The interior experience of exterior environment in Modern architecture has also been extended to include the concept of the urban interior. This has been most clearly articulated by Aldo van Eyck, who held that all inhabited rooms – even exterior rooms – are fundamentally interiors, and argued that all spaces designed by mankind, inside or outside, rooms or streets, must be fundamentally conceived and experienced as interior. In his extensive studies of the cultures of Africa, and in particular of

Dogon villages, Van Eyck noted how mankind 'brought inside what was outside, close what was far, making the universe into an interior – in the form of a basket, a bowl, an urn, a sarcophagus, a house, a temple, a square or a town'. By contrast, Van Eyck was a lifelong critic of Modern urban planning, believing the parallel rows of housing typically employed in these new neighbourhoods produced ill-defined exterior spaces between them, which he called 'hollow space' that provided 'questionable harbor' for inhabitation:

> I am a vehement opponent of current urban planning, which very much hinders spatial boundaries . . . Space has become so continuous that no spaces can be formed . . . we are no longer 'received' by urban squares.

Van Eyck memorably described this deficiency in Modern architecture and urban design: 'Modern architecture has been trying hard to breathe out without breathing in . . . For you can't open up unless you enclose.' This paradoxical insight that openness can only be achieved by way of enclosing related directly to Van Eyck's criticism of 'the contemporary concept (call it sickness) of spatial continuity and the tendency to erase every articulation between spaces', as well as his conception of inhabited spaces as fundamentally interiors:

> For thirty years architecture – not to mention urbanism – has been providing outside for man even inside (aggravating the conflict by attempting to eliminate the essential difference). Architecture (sic urbanism) implies the creation of 'interior' both outside and inside, for 'exterior' is that which precedes man-made environment; that which is counteracted by it; that which is persuaded to become commensurate by being interiorized.[21]

For Van Eyck, the quality of interior experience, whether on the inside or outside of buildings, was all that matters: 'It is not space that counts ultimately, but the *interior* of the space and, above all, the *inner horizon* of that interior – whether it is inside or outside.'[22]

The building shaped entirely by the interior experience of its inhabitants, involving a series of expanding volumes reaching for natural light and the forest, and experienced as an acoustic echo of the Finnish landscape during the ritual of worship. Alvar Aalto, Church of the Three Crosses, Vuoksenniska, Imatra, Finland, interior of sanctuary (top), with section and plan superimposed (bottom); sketch made on 18 September 1983.

Conclusion
Interior Experience as Initiation and Evaluation of Architecture

Interior space and its experience is the fundamental originating inspiration and essential reason-for-being of architecture, as well as the primary determinant of architectural design. It follows directly that the only appropriate way to evaluate architecture is through our experience of it, with particular emphasis on the occupation of interior space. In this understanding, the inhabitational character of interior space should be given primacy in the conception, construing and design of architecture; in the construction and realization of architecture; and in the experience and evaluation of the built work of architecture. This conception centres on the seemingly self-evident recognition that the appropriate enrichment of the interior experience of occupants is the ultimate goal in the design of an architectural work, and that interior spatial experience is the only valid measure of the quality of an inhabited work of architecture.

Yet in the overwhelming majority of existing architectural studies, critical events in the history of architecture, and the buildings that embody them, have most often been scripted in stylistic or purely formal terms – terms that focus on primarily the exterior form, and largely ignore the interior experience. As a result, while the interior experience of buildings is what really matters to those who inhabit them, today the space within is seemingly of less and less interest to many of those who design those same buildings.

This tendency to emphasize the exterior form over the life that takes place in the interior was noted at the beginning of the Modern period by the Irish architect Eileen Gray, who practised her entire life in France. In describing the house she called E.1027, which she designed and constructed for herself and Jean Badovici in 1929 at Roquebrune-Cap-Martin, France, Gray made direct reference to Le Corbusier's ideal of the play of light and shade on the exteriors of masses:

> External architecture seems to have absorbed avant-garde architects at the expense of the interior, as if a house should be conceived for the pleasure of the eye more than for the well-being of its inhabitants. If lyricism can be dedicated to the play of masses brought together in daylight, the interior should respond to human needs and the exigencies of individual life, and it should ensure calm and intimacy . . . The thing constructed is more important than the way it is constructed, and the process is subordinate to the plan, *not the plan to the process*. It is not only a matter of constructing beautiful arrangements of lines, but above all *dwellings for people*.[1]

Gray's critique of the formulaic and formalist tendencies she perceived in early Modern architecture is equally relevant today. Arguing that architectural design must always respond to its specific place and construct the atmosphere necessary to sustain a rich inner life for the inhabitants, rather than follow predetermined and generic formulas, she noted: 'Formulas are nothing; life is everything. And life is simultaneously mind and heart.'[2]

In 1965, the year of Le Corbusier's death, the architectural historian Eduard Sekler echoed Gray's call for architecture (and architectural criticism) to be determined and generated by the life that takes place within it: 'Architectural criticism also has to move in the direction of interpreting architectural experience as a totality

. . . those attempts will be most successful which are nourished from and return to a fullness of being.'[3] Following this insight, we can say that in order to make both appropriate architectural designs, as well as appropriate analyses of the rooms in which we live, another definition of criticism is required – a definition much less concerned with style and form, and much more concerned with the tradition of building, the making of places and the experience of the space within. In this understanding, architecture is concerned much less with a building's external form, and much more with how the space within a building affects what is experienced by those who inhabit it. This would constitute both a more comprehensive and meaningful analysis of the experience of inhabitation, and of the design process that leads to its realization in architecture.

In light of this realization, the approach taken in this book is not based on the usual instruments of academic research, which most often act to distance, rather than bring near, the subject to be engaged. Rather, the approach begins with the actual experiences of interior spaces, and with the understanding that it requires no special training or skills to have an experience – as John Dewey has noted, it is simply and crucially an integral part of everyday life. The intention is to propose a criticism that acts to bind together the perspectives of academics, critics, practitioners and the inhabitants of architecture – precisely because these are almost always considered to be mutually exclusive discourses. Despite all the words that have been and continue to be written about architecture, the actual lived experience of those who inhabit the interior spaces of architecture – the ultimate purpose of the discipline – is almost entirely absent from critical discourses in architectural schools and practices, and in the public realm. This last absence is crucially important, and is without question one of the reasons why the quality and appropriateness of architecture has recently been seen as increasingly irrelevant for those whose daily lives quite literally take place in it.

Alvar Aalto precisely articulated this conception when he stated that what really matters in architecture is not what a building looks like on the day it opens, but rather what the building is like to live in thirty years later. More recently, Steven Holl has argued for a richly layered interior experience that is contrasted and complemented by the simplicity and formal silence of the exterior: 'I really like the muteness of the outside when it comes with the exhilaration of the spaces inside. That's the right proportion with emphasis on the interior experience.'[4] Embracing the primacy of interior experience in architecture involves rediscovering the fundamental ethical principles underlying the process of edification, as was indicated by Aldo van Eyck's critique of the conception of Modern architecture being defined solely by space and time: 'Whatever space and time mean, place and occasion mean more, since space in the image of man is place and time in the image of man is occasion.'[5] Van Eyck held that an event in human life is an occasion; that it takes place in the space within; and that architecture was fundamentally about allowing what he called our 'homecoming' – an essentially interior experience.

Louis Kahn's deep reflections on the nature of architecture, and how its nature should be engaged in his own design process, led to a remarkable, if heretofore overlooked, insight into the relationship between functional programme and architectural design, and the essential part played by interior spatial experience in their realization. Kahn maintained that, contrary to standard practice, architecture does not begin with the functional programme of predetermined space quantities, but rather with an inspiration regarding the nature of the interior space: 'The space induces the project. If you have a space, something happens, the program then starts. It doesn't start before you make the space.'[6] It is both surprising and disappointing that this insight of Kahn's has not been more widely noted and discussed in either practices or schools of architecture, for its implies a reversal of the usual design process, wherein the functional programme is determined well before the interior spaces are conceived. Kahn proposed the exact opposite – that the architect should begin with an idea about the nature of an interior space, a room as the place of experience, and that this interior spatial conception then gives direction and meaning to the development of programme, building design, material selection and site situation.

This book has argued that architectural design must be re-grounded and redefined as primarily about the conception and construction of interior space and its experience – what it is like to live inside the rooms within a building – and not about what the building's exterior form looks like when seen from the outside. In this understanding, architecture at its most profound and fundamental level is primarily concerned not with a building's exterior appearance, but rather with how a building's interior spaces are ordered to house the activities and events that take place within it; how its rooms engage their place and its history of human occupation; how its rooms engage the landscape, climate, and light of their environment; how its rooms are built, how they are structured, and of what materials they are made; and how all these together affect what is experienced by those who inhabit its rooms. Today we need to again rediscover the ancient insight that the interior experience of inhabitation is both the beginning of and inspiration for the process of architectural design, as well as the end and evaluation of every work of architecture.

References

1 The Space Within as the Origin of Architecture

1 The Japanese culture of blackness and shadows is documented in Jun'ichiro Tanizaki, *In Praise of Shadows*, trans. Thomas J. Harper and Edward G. Seidensticker (New Haven, CT, 1977).

2 Frank Lloyd Wright, *An American Architecture* (New York, 1955), pp. 217–19.

3 Ibid., p. 80.

4 Okakura Kakuzō, *The Book of Tea* (Tokyo, 1956), p. 45.

5 John Dewey, *Art as Experience* (New York, 1980), p. 209.

6 Wright, *An American Architecture*, pp. 208–10.

7 Le Corbusier, *Oeuvre complète, 1946–1952*, ed. W. Boesiger (Zurich, 1953), p. 186.

8 Le Corbusier and Jean Petit, *Un couvent de Le Corbusier* (Paris, 1961), p. 20.

9 Le Corbusier, letter to Edgar Varèse, 12 June 1956, Fondation Le Corbusier, g2.20.516–517, quoted in Roberto Gargiani and Anna Rosellini, *Le Corbusier: Béton Brut and Ineffable Space, 1940–1965, Surface Materials and Psychophysiology of Vision* (Lausanne, 2011), p. 465.

10 Louis Kahn, 'The Room, the Street, and Human Agreement' [1971], in *Louis I. Kahn: Writings, Lectures, Interviews*, ed. Alessandra Latour (New York, 1991), p. 263.

11 Louis Kahn, *What Will Be Has Always Been: The Words of Louis I. Kahn*, ed. Richard Saul Wurman (New York, 1991), p. 85.

12 Kahn, 'The Room, the Street, and Human Agreement', p. 265.

13 Kahn, *What Will Be Has Always Been*, p. 248.

14 Kahn, 'The Room, the Street, and Human Agreement', p. 264.

15 Kahn, 'How'm I doing, Corbusier?' [1972], in *Louis I. Kahn: Writings, Lectures, Interviews*, pp. 298–9.

16 Steven Holl, *Steven Holl: Architecture Spoken* (New York, 2007), p. 274.

17 Tod Williams and Billie Tsien, 'What Lasts', lecture given at Washington University in St Louis, Missouri, 30 January 2009; from the author's notes taken at the lecture.

18 Tod Williams and Billie Tsien, quoted in Michael Welton, ed., *Drawing from Practice* (London, 2015), p. 208.

19 Adrian Stokes, 'Smooth and Rough' [1951], in *The Critical Writings of Adrian Stokes* (London, 1978), vol. II, p. 241.

20 Adrian Stokes, 'The Stones of Rimini' [1934], in *The Critical Writings of Adrian Stokes*, vol. I, p. 258.

21 Ibid., p. 235.

22 Adrian Stokes, 'The Invitation in Art' [1965], in *The Critical Writings of Adrian Stokes*, vol. III, p. 277.

23 Adrian Stokes, 'The Stones of Rimini', p. 229.

2 The Nearness of Interior Experience and the Distance of Exterior Form

1 During the 1990s, when I was Director of the School of Architecture at the University of Florida, at the beginning of the school year the 300 new freshman architecture and design students were asked to name their favourite architect, with some 98 per cent typically responding 'Frank Lloyd Wright', and then they were asked if they had ever visited a building designed by that architect, to which only 1 per cent responded in the affirmative – they 'knew' Wright's work only through photographs of it.

2 Alvar Aalto, quoted in Colin St John Wilson, *The Other Tradition of Modern Architecture* (London, 1995), p. 123.

3 Frank Lloyd Wright, 'Reply to Mr Sturgis's Criticism', in *In the Cause of Architecture* (Buffalo, NY, 1909), reprinted in Jack Quinan, *Frank Lloyd Wright's Larkin Building* (Cambridge, MA, 1987), p. 166.

4 Josef Albers, 'On General Education and Art Education', quoted in Mary Emma Harris, *The Arts at Black Mountain College* (Cambridge, MA, 1987), p. 17.

5 Wilfried Wang, 'Architecture as Art', in *Alterstudio Architecture, 6 Houses* (Oxford, OH, 2014), pp. 8–9.

6 Aldo van Eyck, *Aldo van Eyck: Writings*, ed. Vincent Ligtelijn and Francis Strauven (Amsterdam, 2008), vol. I, p. 63.

7 David Van Zanten, 'Kahn and Architectural Composition', unpublished paper read on 24 January 2004, 'Engaging Louis I. Kahn: A Legacy for the Future', conference, 23–24 January 2004, Yale University; courtesy of David Van Zanten.

8 Louis Kahn, quoted in 'Kahn on Beaux-Arts Training', ed. William Jordy, *Architectural Review*, CLV (June 1974), p. 332.

9 Frank Lloyd Wright, *Frank Lloyd Wright: Collected Writings, 1894–1930*, ed. Bruce Brooks Pfeiffer (New York, 1992), vol. I, p. 24; vol. II, p. 205.

10 Ibid., vol. 1, p. 36. Wright later restated this even more explicitly: 'for buildings are the background or framework for the human life within their walls'; Frank Lloyd Wright, *An American Architecture* (New York, 1955), p. 53.

11 Walter Benjamin, 'The Work of Art in the Age of Mechanical Reproduction', in *Illuminations: Walter Benjamin*, ed. Hannah Arendt (New York, 1969), pp. 239–40.

12 Martin Heidegger, 'The Thing', in *Poetry, Language, Thought*, ed. Albert Hofstadter (New York, 1971), pp. 168–9.

13 Juhani Pallasmaa, *The Eyes of the Skin* (London, 1996), p. 10. Pallasmaa followed this first book, an instant classic, with two other equally succinct arguments for all the senses to be re-engaged in architecture; *The Thinking Hand* (2009) and *The Embodied Image* (2011).

14 Ibid., pp. 29, 32.

15 Juhani Pallasmaa, 'On Atmosphere', in *Encounters 2: Juhani Pallasmaa, Architectural Essays*, ed. Peter MacKeith (Helsinki, 2012), p. 239.

16 Juhani Pallasmaa, 'Touching the World', introduction to 2nd edn of *The Eyes of the Skin* (Chichester, 2005), p. 13.

17 Georges Braque, quoted in Serge Fauchereau, *Braque*, trans. Kenneth Lyons (New York, 1987), p. 30.

18 Georges Braque, quoted in Karen Wilkin, *Georges Braque* (New York, 1991), p. 50.

19 Ibid.

20 Ibid., pp. 102–3.

21 Ibid., p. 46.

22 Braque, quoted in Fauchereau, *Braque*, p. 24.

23 John Dewey, *Art as Experience* (New York, 1934), p. 237.

24 Wright, as quoted by his apprentice Bob Mosher in a 1977 letter, in Donald Hoffmann, *Frank Lloyd Wright's Fallingwater* (New York, 1978), p. 17.

25 Wright, in an interview with Hugh Downs, 1953, quoted in Frank Lloyd Wright, *The Future of Architecture* (New York, 1953), p. 16.

26 Kenneth Frampton, *Studies in Tectonic Culture* (Cambridge, MA, 1995), p. 1.

27 Paul Valéry, 'Introduction to the Method of Leonardo', in *Paul Valéry: An Anthology*, selected and intro. by James R. Lawler (Princeton, NJ, 1965), p. 82.

28 Aldo van Eyck, *Aldo van Eyck: Writings*, ed. Vincent Ligtelijn and Francis Strauven (Amsterdam, 2008), vol. 1, p. 548.

3 Three Early Modern Conceptions of Interior Space

1 Frank Lloyd Wright, *In the Cause of Architecture* [1908] (New York, 1975), p. 56. This was published twenty years before Le Corbusier wrote an almost identical definition.

2 Ibid., p. 153.

3 'Woven plan' is a term developed by the author in writings on the three early Modern plan types. This was necessitated by the fact that Wright never gave a name to his Prairie period floor plan type, such as the names *Raumplan* and *plan libre*, coined for Adolf Loos (by his student Kulka) and by Le Corbusier himself, respectively, to identify what they perceived as their contributions to the development of the modern floor plan. While Wright's plan type has sometimes been called 'open plan', openness in Modern planning is not unique to Wright, and is not particularly descriptive of what makes Wright's plans notable.

4 The evolution of all the Prairie house plans from the Wright House was definitively demonstrated by Patrick Pinnell, 'Academic Traditions and Individual Talent' [1991], in *Frank Lloyd Wright: A Primer on Architectural Principles*, ed. Robert McCarter (New York, 1991), and *On and By Frank Lloyd Wright: A Primer of Architectural Principles*, ed. Robert McCarter (London, 2005).

5 John Dewey, *Art as Experience* (New York, 1934), p. 209.

6 Frank Lloyd Wright, *An Autobiography* (New York, 1932), p. 34.

7 Frank Lloyd Wright, *A Testament* (New York, 1957), p. 224.

8 Ibid., p. 220.

9 Frank Lloyd Wright [1925], *The Life-work of Frank Lloyd Wright, Wendingen* (reprinted New York, 1965), p. 57.

10 Frank Lloyd Wright, *Frank Lloyd Wright: Writings and Buildings*, ed. E. Kaufmann Jr and B. Raeburn (New York, 1960), p. 220.

11 This concept was later precisely articulated in the Danish architect Jørn Utzon's essay, 'Platforms and Plateaus: Ideas of a Danish Architect', *Zodiac*, x (1962), pp. 113–41.

12 Wright, *An American Architecture* (New York, 1955), p. 146.

13 Frank Lloyd Wright, *In the Cause of Architecture* [1908] (New York, 1975), p. 153.

14 The word *Raumplan* was first used to describe Loos's design concept by his student Heinrich Kulka, in the first book on Loos's work, *Adolf Loos* (Vienna, 1931). Adolf Loos, quoted in *Raumplan Versus Plan Libre: Adolf Loos and Le Corbusier, 1919–1930*, ed. Max Risselada (Delft, 1988), p. 78.

15 Ibid.

16 Ibid., p. 46.

17 Ibid., p. 141.

18 Adolf Loos, 'The Principle of Cladding' [1898], in *Adolf Loos: Spoken into the Void, Collected Essays, 1897–1900* (Cambridge, 1982), p. 66.

19 Adolf Loos, 'Regarding Economy', in *Raumplan Versus Plan Libre*, ed. Risselada, pp. 137–8.

20 Adolphe Appia, *L'Oeuvre d'art vivant* (Paris, 1921), p. 24, quoted in Jan de Her, *The Architectonic Colour: Polychromy in the Purist Architecture of Le Corbusier* (Rotterdam, 2009), p. 111.

21 Le Corbusier [1930], *Precisions: On the Present State of Architecture and City Planning* (Cambridge, MA, 1991), p. 51.
22 Kenneth Frampton, *Le Corbusier* (London, 2001), p. 79.

4 The Separate Paths of the Eye and the Body in Experience

1   Frank Lloyd Wright, 'In the Cause of Architecture', *Architectural Record* (May 1914), reprinted in *Frank Lloyd Wright: Collected Writings, 1894–1930* (New York, 1992), vol. 1, pp. 129, 127. 'Progress before precedent' was the contemporary slogan of the Architectural League.
2   Ibid., p. 94.
3   Marcel Breuer, *Marcel Breuer: Buildings and Projects, 1921–1961* (New York, 1962), p. 253.
4   Marcel Breuer [1955], in *Marcel Breuer: Sun and Shadow, The Philosophy of an Architect*, ed. Peter Blake (London, 1956), p. 64.
5   Le Corbusier [1923], *Vers une architecture*, trans. Frederick Etchells as *Towards a New Architecture* (New York, 1960), p. 66.
6   Colin Rowe, 'The Mathematics of the Ideal Villa' [1947], in *The Mathematics of the Ideal Villa and Other Essays* (Cambridge, MA, 1976).
7   Henri Bergson, *Time and Free Will*, trans. F. L. Pogson (London, 1913), p. xix.
8   Ibid., pp. 112, 120.
9   Jay Appleton, *The Experience of Landscape* (New York, 1975), pp. 63–7.
10 Grant Hildebrand, *The Wright Space: Pattern and Meaning in Frank Lloyd Wright's Houses* (Seattle, WA, 1991).
11 Vincent Scully, quoted in John Sergeant, 'Frank Lloyd Wright's Use of Movement', in *Architecture and Movement*, ed. Peter Blundell Jones and Mark Meagher (New York, 2015), p. 57.
12 Frank Lloyd Wright, *An American Architecture* (New York, 1955), p. 61.
13 Paul Valéry, *Paul Valéry: Dialogues*, trans. W. M. Stewart (New York, 1956), pp. 89–90, 93.
14 Paul Valéry, *Paul Valéry: An Anthology*, selected and intro. by James R. Lawler (New York, 1956), p. 49.
15 John Berger, 'The Moment of Cubism' [1969], in *John Berger: Selected Essays*, ed. Geoff Dyer (New York, 2001), p. 86.
16 Josef Albers and François Bucher, *Despite Straight Lines* (Cambridge, MA, 1961), p. 52.
17 Colin Rowe and Robert Slutzky, 'Transparency: Literal and Phenomenal' [1956], in *Transparency* (Basel, 1997), p. 22.

5 The Shape of Interior Space and the Boundary of Place

1 Aldo van Eyck, describing the work of Gerrit Rietveld at the time of Rietveld's death, 'The Ball Bounces Back' and 'Squares with a Smile', in *Aldo van Eyck: Writings*, ed. Vincent Ligtelijn and Francis Strauven (Amsterdam, 2008), vol. II, pp. 145–7, 156.

2 Auguste Choisy, *Histoire de l'architecture*, 2 vols (Paris, 1899). Choisy's *Histoire*, so important to the development of modern architecture, has, since the last (1903) edition, almost disappeared.

3 Luigi Moretti, 'Strutture e sequenze di spazi', *Spazio*, VII (December 1952–April 1953), published in English, trans. Thomas Stevens, in *Oppositions*, IV (New York, 1974), pp. 123–39.

4 Ibid., p. 138.

5 Luigi Moretti, 'Structures and Sequences of Spaces', trans. Marina de Conciliis, in *Luigi Moretti: Works and Writings*, ed. Federico Bucci and Marco Mulazzani (New York, 2002), p. 181.

6 Ibid.

7 Peter Magyar, *Spaceprints: A Handbook of Applied Topology in Architecture* (Auburn, AL, 1984).

8 Peter Magyar, *Thought Palaces* (Amsterdam, 1998), p. 11. Magyar's drawing research has continued in *ThinkInk* (Dubuque, IA, 2010) and several other books.

9 Dom Hans van der Laan, *Architectonic Space* (Leiden, 1983), pp. 44, 11–12.

10 Ibid., pp. 12, 15, 16, 18, 63.

11 Carlo Scarpa, 'Furnishings' [1964], in *Carlo Scarpa: The Complete Works*, ed. Francesco Dal Co and Giuseppe Mazzariol (New York, 1984), p. 282.

12 Martin Heidegger, 'Building Dwelling Thinking' [1954], in *Martin Heidegger: Basic Writings*, ed. David F. Krell (New York, 1977), pp. 323, 332.

13 Frank Lloyd Wright, *An American Architecture* (New York, 1955), p. 61.

14 Aldo van Eyck, 'The Inner Horizon in Wright's Imperial Hotel' [1966] and 'On Frank Lloyd Wright's Imperial Hotel' [1968], in *Aldo van Eyck: Writings*, vol. II, pp. 477–8. The second statement was from a letter written to the prime minister of Japan as part of a campaign to save the Imperial Hotel, but it was destroyed later that year to make way for a high-rise hotel.

15 A. S. Eddington, *The Nature of the Physical World* (New York, 1928), p. 83.

16 Roberto Gargiani and Anna Rosellini, *Le Corbusier: Béton Brut and Ineffable Space, 1940–1965, Surface Materials and Psychophysiology of Vision* (Lausanne, 2011), pp. 393–4.

17 Le Corbusier, *Ronchamp* (Zurich, 1957), p. 120.

18 Gargiani and Rosellini, *Le Corbusier: Béton Brut and Ineffable Space*, p. 491.

19 Le Corbusier, *The Modulor* [1948] (Cambridge, MA, 1954), p. 78.
20 Yvonne Farrell, 'Nothing is Something', interview, Ljubljana, Slovenia, *Architect's Bulletin* (December 2009), p. 104.

6 The Society of Spaces and the Emplacement of Encounters

1 Louis Kahn, 'I Love Beginnings' [1972], in *Louis I. Kahn: Writings, Lectures, Interviews*, ed. Alessandra Latour (New York, 1991), p. 291.
2 Louis Kahn, *What Will Be Has Always Been: The Words of Louis I. Kahn*, ed. Richard Saul Wurman (New York, 1986), p. 47.
3 Louis Kahn, quoted in Alexandra Tyng, *Beginnings: Louis I. Kahn's Philosophy of Architecture* (New York, 1984), p. 175.
4 Kahn, 'An Architect Speaks his Mind' [1972], in *Louis I. Kahn: Writings, Lectures, Interviews*, ed. Latour, p. 294.
5 Kahn, 'The Room, the Street, and Human Agreement' [1971], in *Louis I. Kahn: Writings, Lectures, Interviews*, ed. Latour, p. 264.
6 Kahn, 'Spaces Order and Architecture' [1957], in *Louis I. Kahn: Writings, Lectures, Interviews*, ed. Latour, p. 75.
7 Kahn, 'Silence and Light' [1969], in *Louis I. Kahn: Writings, Lectures, Interviews*, ed. Latour, p. 244.
8 Kahn, 'Marin City Redevelopment' [1960], in *Louis I. Kahn: Writings, Lectures, Interviews*, ed. Latour, p. 111.
9 Louis Kahn, transcribed notes of studio discussion, University of Pennsylvania, 5 December 1960; from author's collection.
10 Kahn, 'On Philosophical Horizons' [1960] and 'Form and Design' [1961], in *Louis I. Kahn: Writings, Lectures, Interviews*, ed. Latour, pp. 10, 116.
11 Kahn, 'A Statement' [1962], in *Louis I. Kahn: Writings, Lectures, Interviews*, ed. Latour, p. 152.
12 Kahn, *What Will Be Has Always Been*, pp. 202–3.
13 Kahn, 'Talks with Students' [1964], in *Louis I. Kahn: Writings, Lectures, Interviews*, ed. Latour, p. 164.
14 Luis Barragán, quoted by Kahn, 'Silence' [1968], in *Louis I. Kahn: Writings, Lectures, Interviews*, ed. Latour, p. 233.
15 Kahn, 'Remarks' [1965], in *Louis I. Kahn: Writings, Lectures, Interviews*, ed. Latour, p. 206.
16 Louis Kahn, *Louis Kahn in Conversation: Interviews with John W. Cook and Heinrich Klotz*, ed. Jules D. Prown and Karen E. Denavit (New Haven, CT, 2015), p. 167.
17 Ibid., p. 71.
18 Kahn, *What Will Be Has Always Been*, p. 257.
19 Ibid., p. 79.

20 Louis Kahn, 'Princeton 1961', lecture, Box 65, LIK Collection; quoted in
   Sarah Goldhagen, *Louis Kahn's Situated Modernism* (New Haven,
   CT, 2001), p. 198.
21 Kahn, 'Form and Design' [1961], in *Louis I. Kahn: Writings, Lectures,
   Interviews*, ed. Latour, p. 114.
22 Gail Satler, *Frank Lloyd Wright's Living Space* (Dekalb, IL, 1999),
   pp. xii, 8, 12, 110, 114.
23 Ibid., pp. 81, 82.
24 Robin Evans, 'Figures, Doors and Passages', in *Translations from
   Drawing to Building and Other Essays* (Cambridge, MA, 1997), p. 56.
25 Ibid., pp. 69, 87, 79, 85.
26 Ibid., pp. 88–90.

7 The Nesting of Places at Once Intimate and Immense

1 Gaston Bachelard, *The Poetics of Space* [1958], first published in English
   in 1964, trans. Maria Jolas (Boston, MA, 1969).
2 Ibid., pp. xxxiv, 3, 7, 15.
3 Ibid., pp. 17, 22, 37.
4 Georges Spyridaki, *Morte lucide* (Paris, 1953), p. 35, quoted in Bachelard,
   The Poetics of Space, p. 51.
5 Bachelard, *The Poetics of Space*, pp. 47, 85–6, 88, 107.
6 Ibid., pp. 90–91; quote is from Victor Hugo, *Notre-Dame de Paris*
   (1832 restored edition), Book IV, Chapter 3.
7 Bachelard, *The Poetics of Space*, pp. 101, 131.
8 Ibid., pp. 136, 146, 171, 174.
9 Herman Hertzberger, *The Future of Architecture* (Rotterdam, 2013),
   p. 55.
10 Bachelard, *The Poetics of Space*, pp. 186, 203.
11 Ralph Waldo Emerson, *Emerson: Essays and Lectures* (New York, 1983),
   p. 487.
12 Bachelard, *The Poetics of Space*, pp. 190, 193.
13 Ibid., pp. 215, 108, 218, 217, 226.
14 Ibid., p. 215.
15 Edward T. Hall, *The Hidden Dimension* (New York, 1966), p. 51.
16 Harry Mallgrave, *The Architect's Brain: Neuroscience, Creativity and
   Architecture* (Chichester, 2010), pp. 149, 151. Among the works cited by
   Mallgrave are Semir Zeki, *Inner Vision: An Exploration of Art and the
   Brain* (Oxford, 1999), and 'The Neurology of Ambiguity,' *Consciousness
   and Cognition*, XIII/1 (March 2004).
17 Wright, *An American Architecture* (New York, 1955), p. 194.
18 John Dewey, *Art as Experience* (New York, 1934), p. 213.

19 Leon Battista Alberti, *On the Art of Building*, Book 1, Part 9 (Cambridge, MA, 1988), p. 23.
20 Peter Zumthor, *Thinking Architecture* (Basel, 2006), pp. 22, 72.
21 Vittorio Gregotti, *Inside Architecture* (Cambridge, MA, 1996), pp. 70–71.
22 Michael Cadwell, 'Swimming at the Querini Stampalia', in *Strange Details* (Cambridge, MA, 2007), p. 12.
23 Peter Noever, 'Reminiscences', in *Carlo Scarpa: The Other City / Die Andere Stadt* (Berlin, 1989), p. 8.

8 Making Room for Experience and Memory

1 Edward Hall, *The Hidden Dimension* (New York, 1969), pp. 106–7.
2 Juhani Pallasmaa, 'The Rooms of Memory', in *Understanding Architecture: A Primer on Architecture as Experience*, ed. Robert McCarter and Juhani Pallasmaa (London, 2012), p. 257.
3 Pallasmaa, 'Memory and the Lifeworld', in *Understanding Architecture*, p. 329.
4 Arnaud quote is from Bachelard, *The Poetics of Space*, trans. Maria Jolas (Boston, MA, 1969), p. 137; Pallasmaa, *Understanding Architecture*, p. 331.
5 Henri Bergson, *Matter and Memory* [1908 edn], trans. N. M. Paul and W. S. Palmer (New York, 1988), pp. 31, 81.
6 Ibid., pp. 138–9, 233.
7 Edward S. Casey, *Remembering: A Phenomenological Study* [1987] (Bloomington, IN, 2000), p. 172.
8 Edmund Husserl, *Experience and Judgement*, quoted ibid., p. 181.
9 Casey, *Remembering*, pp. 182, 186; Casey references Aristotle, *Physics*, 212a 28–31 (Ross translation).
10 Casey, *Remembering*, pp. 190, 193, 197, 215.
11 Frank Lloyd Wright, 'The Meaning of Materials – Glass: In the Cause of Architecture', essay written for *Architectural Record* (July 1928), in *In the Cause of Architecture*, ed. F. Gutheim (New York, 1975), pp. 197, 202.
12 Robert Pogue Harrison, *Forests: Shadows of Civilization* (Chicago, IL, 1992), p. 232.
13 Ibid., pp. 233–5.
14 Le Corbusier, *Urbanisme* (Paris, 1925), p. 174. This phrase was changed in the later English translation, where instead of 'Loos' it says 'A friend'; this noted by Beatriz Colomina, *Privacy and Publicity* (Cambridge, MA, 1994), p. 234, note on p. 369.
15 Colomina, *Privacy and Publicity*, p. 234.
16 Louis Kahn, quoted in Henry Plummer, *Masters of Light* (Tokyo, 2003), p. 195.
17 Louis Kahn, *Light is the Theme* (Fort Worth, TX, 1975), p. 12.

18 Le Corbusier, *Une petite maison* (Zurich, 1954), pp. 22–3.

19 Diana Fuss, *The Sense of an Interior: Four Writers and the Rooms that Shaped Them* (London, 2004), pp. 2, 151, 19, 154.

20 Marilyn Chandler, *Dwelling in the Text: Houses in American Fiction* (Berkeley, CA, 1991), pp. 31, 157, 179. Henry David Thoreau, *Walden; or, Life in the Woods* (New York, 1985), pp. 434–5.

21 Rainer Maria Rilke, *The Notebook of Malte Laurids Brigge* (London, 1930), pp. 24, 44.

22 Simon Mawer, *The Glass Room* (New York, 2009), pp. 3–4, 404.

23 André Breton, *Nadja* [1928], trans. Richard Howard (New York, 1960), p. 18.

24 Curzio Malaparte, *Fughe in Prigione* (Escapes in Prison) (Milan, 1943), foreword to 2nd edition.

25 Curzio Malaparte, *The Skin* [1949], trans. David Moore (New York, 2013), p. 207.

9 Interior Experience of the Exterior Environment

1 Aldo van Eyck [1962], in *Aldo van Eyck: Writings*, ed. Vincent Ligtelijn and Francis Strauven (Amsterdam, 2008), vol. 1, p. 24.

2 Frank Lloyd Wright, *The Natural House* (New York, 1954), p. 44.

3 Frank Lloyd Wright, *In the Cause of Architecture* [1908], ed. F. Gutheim (New York, 1975), p. 60.

4 Wright, *The Natural House*, p. 106.

5 Ibid., p. 150.

6 Ibid., pp. 46–7.

7 Ibid., pp. 175–9.

8 Frank Lloyd Wright, *The Future of Architecture* (New York, 1953), p. 69.

9 Ibid., pp. 121–3.

10 Reyner Banham, *The Architecture of the Well-tempered Environment* (Chicago, IL, 1969), p. 121.

11 John Dewey, *Art as Experience* (New York, 1934), pp. 15, 193, 220, 230, 213.

12 Gaston Bachelard, *The Poetics of Space*, trans. Maria Jolas (Boston, MA, 1969), p. 216.

13 Alvar Aalto, 'From Doorstep to Living Room', in *Alvar Aalto in his Own Words*, ed. Göran Schildt (New York, 1997), pp. 50–53.

14 David Leatherbarrow, 'Space In and Out of Architecture', in *Architecture Oriented Otherwise* (New York, 2009), p. 267.

15 Leatherbarrow, 'Breathing Walls', in *Architecture Oriented Otherwise*, p. 34.

16 David Leatherbarrow, *Uncommon Ground* (Cambridge, MA, 2000), pp. 55, 176, 183, 186.

17 Le Corbusier, *Precisions* (Cambridge, MA, 1991), pp. 77, 78.

18 Beatriz Colomina, *Privacy and Publicity* (Cambridge, MA, 1994), p. 334.
19 Le Corbusier, March 1951, note in sketchbook E19, No. 398, Fondation Le Corbusier; quoted in Roberto Gargiani and Anna Rosellini, *Le Corbusier: Béton Brut and Ineffable Space, 1940–1965, Surface Materials and Psychophysiology of Vision* (Lausanne, 2011), p. 288.
20 Juhani Pallasmaa, 'The Limits of Architecture', in *Encounters 2: Juhani Pallasmaa, Architectural Essays*, ed. Peter MacKeith (Helsinki, 2012), p. 197.
21 Aldo van Eyck, *Aldo van Eyck: Writings*, vol. II, pp. 571, 118, 319.
22 Aldo van Eyck, *Aldo van Eyck: Works*, ed. Vincent Ligtelijn (Basel, 1999), p. 201.

Conclusion: Interior Experience as Initiation and Evaluation of Architecture

1 Eileen Gray and Jean Badovici, 'Maison en bord de mer', *L'Architecture Vivante* (Winter 1929), translated and reprinted in Caroline Constant, *Eileen Gray* (London, 2000), p. 240.
2 Ibid., p. 239.
3 Eduard Sekler, 'Structure, Construction, Tectonics', in *Structure in Art and Science*, ed. Gyorgy Kepes (New York, 1965), p. 95.
4 Steven Holl, *Steven Holl: Architecture Spoken* (New York, 2007), p. 275.
5 Aldo van Eyck, *Aldo van Eyck: Writings*, ed. Vincent Ligtelijn and Francis Strauven (Amsterdam, 2008), vol. I, p. 49.
6 Louis Kahn (1972), in *What Will Be Has Always Been: The Words of Louis I. Kahn*, ed. Richard Saul Wurman (New York, 1986), p. 178.

Bibliography

Aalto, Alvar, *Alvar Aalto in His Own Words*, ed. Göran Schildt (New York, 1997)
Adorno, Theodor, *Minima Moralia* (London, 1974)
Amaldi, Paolo, *Espaces* (Paris, 2007)
Appleton, Jay, *The Experience of Landscape* (New York, 1975)
Arendt, Hannah, *The Human Condition* (Chicago, IL, 1958)
Arnheim, Rudolf, *The Dynamics of Architectural Form* (Berkeley, CA, 1977)
Bachelard, Gaston, *The Poetics of Space*, trans. Maria Jolas (Boston, MA, 1969)
Baltanás, José, *Walking Through Le Corbusier* (London, 2005)
Banham, Reyner, *The Architecture of the Well-tempered Environment*
    (Chicago, IL, 1969)
Benjamin, Walter, *Illuminations*, ed. Hannah Arendt (New York, 1969)
Berger, John, *John Berger: Selected Essays*, ed. Geoff Dyer (New York, 2001)
Bergson, Henri, *Matter and Memory* [1908 edn], trans. N. M. Paul and
    W. S. Palmer (New York, 1988)
—, *Time and Free Will*, trans. F. L. Pogson (London, 1913)
Blau, Eve, and Nancy Troy, eds, *Architecture and Cubism* (Cambridge, MA, 2002)
Breton, André, *Nadja*, trans. Richard Howard (New York, 1960)
Breuer, Marcel, *Marcel Breuer: Sun and Shadow, The Philosophy of an Architect*,
    ed. Peter Blake (London, 1956)
Caan, Shashi, *Rethinking Design and Interiors: Human Beings in the Built
    Environment* (London, 2011)
Cadwell, Michael, *Strange Details* (Cambridge, MA, 2007)
Casey, Edward S., *Getting Back Into Place: Toward a Renewed Understanding
    of the Place-world* (Bloomington, IN, 1993)
—, *Remembering: A Phenomenological Study* (Bloomington, IN, 2000)
Chandler, Marilyn, *Dwelling in the Text: Houses in American Fiction*
    (Berkeley, CA, 1991)
Choisy, Auguste, *Histoire de l'architecture*, 2 vols (Paris, 1899)
Cohen, Jean-Louis, and Staffan Ahrenberg, eds, *Le Corbusier's Secret Laboratory:
    From Painting to Architecture* (Ostfildern, 2013)

Collins, Peter, *Changing Ideals in Modern Architecture* (Montreal, 1967)

Colomina, Beatriz, *Privacy and Publicity* (Cambridge, MA, 1994)

Creagh, Lucy, Helena Kålberg and Barbara Miller Lane, eds, *Modern Swedish Design: Three Founding Texts* (New York, 2008)

Dewey, John, *Art as Experience* (New York, 1934)

Evans, Robin, *The Projective Cast: Architecture and its Three Geometries* (Cambridge, MA, 1995)

—, *Translations from Drawing to Building and Other Essays* (Cambridge, MA, 1997)

Frampton, Kenneth, *Le Corbusier* (London, 2001)

—, *Studies in Tectonic Culture* (Cambridge, 1995)

Fryer, Judith, *Felicitous Space: The Imaginative Structures of Edith Wharton and Willa Cather* (Chapel Hill, NC, 1986)

Fuss, Diana, *The Sense of an Interior: Four Writers and the Rooms that Shaped Them* (London, 2004)

Gargiani, Roberto, and Anna Rosellini, *Le Corbusier: Béton Brut and Ineffable Space, 1940–1965, Surface Materials and Psychophysiology of Vision* (Lausanne, 2011)

Gibson, James J., *The Ecological Approach to Visual Perception* (New York, 2015)

Giedion, Sigfried, *Space, Time and Architecture: The Growth of a New Tradition* (Cambridge, MA, 1941)

Grabow, Stephen, and Kent Spreckelmeyer, *The Architecture of Use: Aesthetics and Function in Architectural Design* (New York, 2015)

Gregotti, Vittorio, *Inside Architecture* (Cambridge, MA, 1996)

Hall, Edward, *The Hidden Dimension* (New York, 1966)

Harries, Karsten, *The Ethical Function of Architecture* (Cambridge, MA, 1997)

Harris, Mary Emma, *The Arts at Black Mountain College* (Cambridge, 1987)

Harrison, Robert Pogue, *Forests: Shadows of Civilization* (Chicago, IL, 1992)

Heidegger, Martin, *Martin Heidegger: Basic Writings*, ed. David F. Krell (New York, 1977)

—, *Poetry, Language, Thought*, trans. Martin Hofstadter (New York, 1971)

Her, Jan de, *The Architectonic Colour: Polychromy in the Purist Architecture of Le Corbusier* (Rotterdam, 2009)

Hertzberger, Herman, *Architecture and Structuralism: The Ordering of Space* (Rotterdam, 2015)

—, *Lessons for Students of Architecture* (Rotterdam, 1991)

—, *Space and the Architect: Lessons in Architecture 2* (Rotterdam, 2000)

—, *Space and Learning: Lessons in Architecture 3* (Rotterdam, 2008)

Hildebrand, Grant, *The Wright Space: Pattern and Meaning in Frank Lloyd Wright's Houses* (Seattle, WA, 1991)

Holl, Steven, *Steven Holl: Architecture Spoken* (New York, 2007)

—, Juhani Pallasmaa and Alberto Perez-Gomez, *Questions of Perception: Phenomenology in Architecture* (Tokyo, 1994)

Jones, Peter Blundell, and Mark Meagher, eds, *Architecture and Movement*
    (New York, 2015)
Kahn, Louis, *Light is the Theme* (Fort Worth, TX, 1975)
Latour, Alessandra, ed., *Louis I. Kahn: Writings, Lectures, Interviews*
    (New York, 1991)
Le Corbusier, *Creation is a Patient Search* (New York, 1960)
—, *Precisions: On the Present State of Architecture and City Planning*,
    trans. Edith S. Aujame (Cambridge, MA, 1991)
—, *Towards a New Architecture*, trans. Frederick Etchells (New York, 1960)
—, *The Modulor*, trans. Peter de Francia and Anna Bostock
    (Cambridge, MA, 1954)
—, *Urbanisme* (Paris, 1925), published in English as *The City of To-Morrow
    and Its Planning*, trans. Frederick Etchells (New York, 1929)
Leatherbarrow, David, *Architecture Oriented Otherwise* (New York, 2009)
—, *Uncommon Ground* (Cambridge, MA, 2000)
Ligtelijn, Vincent, ed., *Aldo van Eyck: Works* (Basel, 1999)
—, and Francis Strauven, eds, *Aldo van Eyck: Writings*, vol. I: *The Child, The City
    and the Artist* (Amsterdam, 2008)
—, *Aldo van Eyck: Writings*, vol. II: *Collected Articles and Other Writings,
    1947–1998* (Amsterdam, 2008)
Loos, Adolf, *Adolf Loos: Spoken into the Void, Collected Essays, 1897–1900*
    (Cambridge, MA, 1982)
Magyar, Peter, *Spaceprints: A Handbook of Applied Topology in Architecture*
    (Auburn, AL, 1984)
Malaparte, Curzio, *The Skin*, trans. David Moore (New York, 2013)
Mallgrave, Harry Francis, *The Architect's Brain: Neuroscience, Creativity and
    Architecture* (Chichester, 2010)
Malnar, Joy Monice, and Frank Vodvarka, *Sensory Design* (Minneapolis,
    MN, 2004)
Malpas, J. E., *Place and Experience: A Philosophical Topography*
    (Cambridge, 1999)
Mawer, Simon, *The Glass Room* (New York, 2009)
McCarter, Robert, *Aalto* (London, 2014)
—, *Aldo van Eyck* (New Haven, CT, 2015)
—, *Carlo Scarpa* (London, 2013)
—, *Frank Lloyd Wright* (London, 1997)
—, *Louis I. Kahn* (London, 2005)
—, ed., *On and By Frank Lloyd Wright: A Primer of Architectural Principles*
    (London, 2005)
—, and Juhani Pallasmaa, *Understanding Architecture: A Primer on Architecture
    as Experience* (London, 2012)
Merleau-Ponty, Maurice, *Phenomenology of Perception*, trans. Colin Smith
    (London, 1962)

Moretti, Luigi, *Luigi Moretti: Works and Writings*, ed. Federico Bucci and Marco
    Mulazzani (New York, 2002)
Neutra, Richard, *Survival through Design* (London, 1954)
Okakura Kakuzō, *The Book of Tea* (Tokyo, 1956)
Pallasmaa, Juhani, *Encounters: Juhani Pallasmaa, Architectural Essays*, ed. Peter
    MacKeith (Helsinki, 2005)
—, *Encounters 2: Juhani Pallasmaa, Architectural Essays*, ed. Peter MacKeith
    (Helsinki, 2012)
—, *The Embodied Image* (Chichester, 2011)
—, *The Eyes of the Skin* (London, 1996)
—, *The Thinking Hand* (Chichester, 2009)
Pfeiffer, Bruce Brooks, ed., *Frank Lloyd Wright: Collected Writings*, vol. I:
    1894–1930 (New York, 1992)
—, *Frank Lloyd Wright: Collected Writings*, vol. II: *1930–1932* (New York, 1992)
—, *Frank Lloyd Wright: Collected Writings*, vol. III: *1931–1939* (New York, 1993)
—, *Frank Lloyd Wright: Collected Writings*, vol. IV: *1939–1949* (New York, 1994)
—, *Frank Lloyd Wright: Collected Writings*, vol. V: *1949–1959* (New York, 1995)
Proun, Jules D., and Karen E. Denavit, eds, *Louis Kahn in Conversation:
    Interviews with John W. Cook and Heinrich Klotz* (New Haven, CT, 2015)
Quinan, Jack, *Frank Lloyd Wright's Larkin Building* (Cambridge, 1987)
Rasmussen, Stein Eiler, *Experiencing Architecture* (Cambridge, MA, 1959)
Rilke, Rainer Maria, *The Notebook of Malte Laurids Brigge* (London, 1930)
Risselada, Max, ed., *Raumplan Versus Plan Libre: Adolf Loos and Le Corbusier,
    1919–1930* (Delft, 1988)
Robinson, Sarah, *Nesting: Body, Dwelling, Mind* (San Francisco, CA, 2011)
Samuel, Flora, *Le Corbusier and the Architectural Promenade* (Basel, 2010)
Satler, Gail, *Frank Lloyd Wright's Living Space* (DeKalb, IL, 1999)
Stokes, Adrian, *The Critical Writings of Adrian Stokes*, vol. I: *1930–1937*
    (London, 1978)
—, *The Critical Writings of Adrian Stokes*, vol. II: *1937–1958* (London, 1978)
—, *The Critical Writings of Adrian Stokes*, vol. III: *1955–1967* (London, 1978)
Tanizaki, Jun'ichiro, *In Praise of Shadows*, trans. Thomas J. Harper and Edward
    G. Seidensticker (New Haven, CT, 1977)
Taylor, Mark, and Julie Ann Preston, *Intimus: Interior Design Theory Reader*
    (Chichester, 2006)
Thoreau, Henry David, *Walden; or, Life in the Woods* (New York, 1985)
Troy, Nancy J., *The De Stijl Environment* (Cambridge, MA, 1983)
Tuan, Yi-Fu, *Space and Place: The Perspective of Experience*
    (Minneapolis, MN, 1977)
Tyng, Alexandra, *Beginnings: Louis I. Kahn's Philosophy of Architecture*
    (New York, 1984)
Utzon, Jorn, 'Platforms and Plateaus: Ideas of a Danish Architect', *Zodiac*,
    X (1962), pp. 113–41

Valéry, Paul, *Paul Valéry: An Anthology*, selected and intro. by James R. Lawler
    (Princeton, NJ, 1965)
—, *Paul Valéry: Dialogues*, trans. W. M. Stewart (New York, 1956)
Van der Laan, Dom Hans, *Architectonic Space* (Leiden, 1983)
Weinthal, Lois, *Toward a New Interior: An Anthology of Interior Design Theory*
    (New York, 2011)
Wilkin, Karen, *Georges Braque* (New York, 1991)
Wilson, Colin St John, *The Other Tradition of Modern Architecture*
    (London, 1995)
Wright, Frank Lloyd, *An American Architecture* (New York, 1955)
—, *An Autobiography* (New York, 1932)
—, *The Future of Architecture* (New York, 1953)
—, *In the Cause of Architecture* (New York, 1975)
—, *The Natural House* (New York, 1954)
—, *A Testament* (New York, 1957)
Wurman, Richard Saul, ed., *What Will Be Has Always Been: The Words of Louis
    I. Kahn* (New York, 1991)
Zevi, Bruno, *Architecture as Space* (New York, 1957)
Zumthor, Peter, *Atmospheres* (Basel, 2006)
—, *Thinking Architecture* (Basel, 2006)

Acknowledgements

In hindsight, it is apparent that I have been preparing myself to write this book since becoming a practising architect and teacher of architecture. I first became aware of the importance of the interior spatial and experiential conception as generative when studying the work of Frank Lloyd Wright, whose idea of 'the space within' I have adopted as the title of this book. My initial articulation of the concept of interior spatial experience as the origin of Wright's architectural designs came in the first of three essays published in the early 1990s in *Global Architecture: Houses*, titled 'Folded Space, Boundless Place: The Houses of Frank Lloyd Wright, Part 1: 1895–1915' This was closely paralleled by the development in 1991 of an initiatory studio project for first-year Master of Architecture students at the University of Florida, which involved the design of a complexly programmed room to be assessed solely on the basis of the interior experience of the inhabitants, rather than on its external form. I want to fondly acknowledge the intensely engaging pedagogical discussions involved in the crafting of that initial studio project, which I undertook with my colleagues Martin Gundersen, Nina Hofer, Robert MacLeod and William Tilson in the summer of 1991. As my now over one thousand former and current design studio students can attest, I have been employing variations on that first 'room' project as the initial exercise in all my graduate and undergraduate studios taught in the 25 years since.

My evolving focus on the generative nature of the interior spatial conception in architectural design, and the importance of interior experience in the evaluation of architecture, was first noted by another colleague at the University of Florida, Caroline Constant, in her introduction of me prior to my giving a lecture to her senior course in history and theory. This conception has been reinforced in later years by my studies of the works of modern architects such as Alvar Aalto, Aldo van Eyck, Carlo Scarpa, Marcel Breuer and, in particular, Louis Kahn, who believed 'the room is the beginning of architecture', and the works of contemporary architects such as Wiel Arets, who argues for the importance of what he calls 'interiority'; Steven Holl, who insists on designing 'with emphasis on the interior experience'; and Kathryn Dean, whose spaces are conceived through 'the excavation of use', resulting in what I have called 'the topographic section'. I want to acknowledge the excellent work of Vivian Constantinopoulos, editorial director at Reaktion Books, who worked with me on my first books on Frank Lloyd Wright throughout the 1990s, when she was with Phaidon Press. Finally, I want to acknowledge the continued support, energetic encouragement and gentle provocations of Juhani Pallasmaa, with whom I authored a book we intended to title *Architecture as Experience*, in homage to John Dewey's *Art as Experience*, and Tod Williams and Billie Tsien, who believe that 'what lasts' in architecture is the interior space, and that buildings are important in our lives 'because of the interior'.

Index

Printed and bound by CPI Group (UK) Ltd, Croydon, CR0 4YY

07/07/2026

14916212-0001

THE SPACE WITHIN